DISTANCE AND DIRECTION

ACKNOWLEDGMENTS

THE GEORGIA REVIEW: "Out of Place," and "Distance and Direction" (nominated for a National Magazine Award in 1999 and listed in "Notable Essays" in *Best American Essays 1999*). PRAIRIE SCHOONER: in a slightly longer version, "Fred Astaire's Hands" (listed in "Notable Essays" in *Best American Essays 1998*). GREEN MOUNTAINS REVIEW: "Bahia de Todos os Santos" (under the title "Octet: Brazil"). GREAT RIVER REVIEW: "Displacement," "White Mountains," "Kerry," "Sonora," "Yellow," "Red," "Green" (under the title sequence "Landscapes"), and "Standard Time." THE SENECA REVIEW: "Blue," and "Lacrimosa" (as part of the 30th Anniversary Issue). WATER • STONE: "Still Life with Flowers." THE OHIO REVIEW: "Requiem," "Richland," "Cedar Breaks," and "Port Townsend" (under the title "Three Landscapes," reprinted in the 30th Anniversary Issue and listed in "Notable Essays" in *Best American Essays 2000*). CHELSEA: "Mix and Match." ASCENT: "Proportion." THE LAUREL REVIEW: "Distance." RIVER TEETH: "Direction."

JUDITH KITCHEN

DISTANCE AND DIRECTION

COFFEE HOUSE PRESS

MINNEAPOLIS

COFFEE HOUSE PRESS is an independent nonprofit literary publisher supported in part by a grant provided by the Minnesota State Arts Board, through an appropriation by the Minnesota State Legislature, and in part by a grant from the National Endowment for the Arts. Significant support was received for this project through a grant from the National Endowment for the Arts, a federal agency, and the Jerome Foundation. Support has also been provided by Athwin Foundation; the Bush Foundation; Buuck Family Foundation; Elmer L. & Eleanor J. Andersen Foundation; Honeywell Foundation; James R. Thorpe Foundation; Lila Wallace-Reader's Digest Fund; McKnight Foundation; Patrick and Aimee Butler Family Foundation; The St. Paul Companies Foundation, Inc.; the law firm of Schwegman, Lundberg, Woessner & Kluth, P.A.; Star Tribune Foundation; the Target Foundation; Wells Fargo Foundation Minnesota; West Group; and many individual donors. To you and our many readers across the country, we send our thanks for your continuing support.

COFFEE HOUSE PRESS books are available to the trade through our primary distributor, Consortium Book Sales & Distribution, 1045 Westgate Drive, Saint Paul, MN 55114. For personal orders, catalogs, or other information, write to: Coffee House Press, 27 North Fourth Street, Suite 400, Minneapolis, MN 55401.

LIBRARY OF CONGRESS CIP INFORMATION
Kitchen, Judith.
Distance and direction / Judith Kitchen.
p. cm.
ISBN 1-56689-121-3 (alk. paper)
I. Title.
PS3561.I845 D57 2001
814'.54--DC21
2001032481

CONTENTS

Remembering with deepest respect
Stanley W. Lindberg, 1939-2000,
with gratitude for all his friendship and support.

I'd also like to thank my family—Robin, Matthew,
William, George—and all the brave people in my
group at Quartz Mountain, Oklahoma.

Once again, for Stan Rubin, who shares these spaces.

In memoriam
Robert B. Randels, 1911–1995

What happened is a wonder, though memory is always incomplete, like a map with places missing. But it's all right, it's entered the imagination and nothing is ever the same.
——DERMOT HEALY, *The Bend for Home*

PREFACE

THE ESSAYS in my first collection, *Only the Dance,* were about time. These are essays of place—of distance and direction and the way memory works through and within landscape. They touch on my personal story (family, travels, home), our national history (the journals of Lewis and Clark, the sinking of a steamboat on the Missouri, the bombing of the Murrah building in Oklahoma City), and a long legacy of violence—the kind of violence that alters place and forges history—at home, in Vietnam, in Brazil and Ireland, and most recently in Macedonia. The long personal essays are really a study in displacement, punctuated by a number of short lyrics that explore method and mood. Woven throughout is a series of elegies for my father. These are the places to which we return, and the ones to which we can never return—where the past and the future collide in increasingly complicated ripples to include the concentric circles of the present.

—JUDITH KITCHEN

BLUE

BUT BLUE IS ROUND. OBOE BLUE. ORB BLUE. EYES.

My father's eyes, ice in the center. Steel, or something more durable than steel. Still, they could burst into laughter. Flame. Heal-all blue, though in the end they clouded, didn't heal. Blue you could hear, even over the phone. Shards of sound. Train whistles fading into black.

My mother's eyes. Vague, star-like. Hidden blue, like the cottony inside of a quilt, shadow on snow, something tucked under, tucked in. Evasive blue, fueled by my grandmother's dark brown secrets. Fueled by my grandfather's sky touching down on each corner of the farm, flat and terminal.

Or my brother George. Laser blue. Strident, say-what-you-mean blue. You can look away, but they will follow. The shortest distance between two points, hypotenuse blue.

William. Wide awake, 5:40 A.M. blue, taking-in-the-world-for-the-first-time cobalt blue. Even then, so clearly mine and not-mine, as though the world had claimed him first with all its shapes, its yellows and greens like little flags catching his attention.

And Matthew. Evening blue, gray at the edges. Sleepy, pulling back into itself as though in contemplation. Whatever we were going to mean to him, it could wait. Music, that's what those eyes contained. A complex chord. Cut through with its own logic.

Radiant energy of wavelength approximately 475 nanometers. Out of the blue: a memory. A membrane of memory, tasting of brine.

Geometry. Mr. Kershner's class, our desks in straight rows. Square. On the board, our careful triangles, each angle quantified, right, oblique, obtuse. Everything adds up. A fact or two. Everything you need to fill in the blanks. So tidy. Spread the arms of the compass. Circles come out where they start. Set them spinning. Generate a sphere. An algebra. A calculus. The world in three dimensions. Rational. Rote.

But life is unruly. Everything spills into everything else. Nothing as clear and cold and perfect as the swirled marble in my hand. Nothing without asking something back. So what does he mean, equally? What does he mean, abstract? They march in playing an old tune, a sad song, Hey Jude, to make it better. Might as well have said *red* and *rectangle.* I wouldn't have flown into this mess of recollection. Might as well have opened my heart to let the trapezoids fly out on their huge, iridescent wings.

Past-tense blue, those Morphos. Time still counting on its fingers. The eyes of a man I might have loved, did love, do, though now that's caught in its own abstraction, its would-haves if not for other circumstances, its keep-the-moment-intact blue that signals a craving for perfection. Perfect blue, without a hint of future. Past perfect.

FRED ASTAIRE'S HANDS

CLEAR DAYS. MEMORY OF WEATHER. WE'RE DRIVING aimlessly west on 104, along The Ridge—a shelf of land about twenty miles deep that runs for over two hundred miles along the southern shore of Lake Ontario. The land here is flat. But the apple orchards tell us it is upstate New York. All summer we've watched: white blossom, nubbin, pale green moon. It takes a lifetime of learning to distinguish darkest fruit from darker leaves. The eye adjusts and suddenly there they are: brilliant, burnished red.

Turning south on an unmarked road, we drive past fields of spent corn. Some farmers will cut their fields, leaving sharp stubble to poke through early snow. Others will let their fields stand as stalks turn paper-thin and dry to the color of parchment. If we kept going, we would cross into Livingston County where much of the country's onions are grown. Black dirt sucking in the light. Further south, potatoes. But here, on the first Sunday in October, cabbage smothers the ground with that particular gray-green color—dusk-color of muted silk—that you can only refer to, when you see it somewhere else, as the color of cabbage.

These landscapes are not beautiful, exactly. They withdraw into themselves, sealed in silence like old men who know more than they will tell you. Even the prosperous farms sprawl across the land with a cluster of ugly sheds and rusted equipment. When you learn to love a land like this, you don't want to be fickle. You take your time, season after season, driving the back roads, letting them tug you forward into the mystery of where people settle.

Or they tug you back to the Southern Tier where you grew up in hills that stretched forever, into Pennsylvania and beyond. That's how far you've come: ninety miles north, to where the land is flat and boring. It took you years to do it—years and two foreign countries and several states—but now you're home. You know you're home because the sumac and milkweed pods and burdock feel so familiar you could walk out into the brush and climb back into the car picking off the sticktights of your childhood.

And when does the "you"—the person who inhabited that childhood—become the "I" of the present, the one who sits, now, in the passenger seat? Here she is, as the fields drift by. Here she is: here I am. But I am passive compared to the child who lifted and touched, who fingered the milkweed and let it fly. I open the window to let the cool air remind me of the day, the hour, the season we've entered.

Suddenly we're bombarded by signs for tax-free cigarettes. Kools. Lucky Strikes. And a diner—at least it looks like a diner—called Sah-Da-Ko-Nee's. Of course we have to stop. Of course we have to discover where we are.

Where we are is the Tonawanda Indian Reservation, one of several small areas of land across upstate New York set aside for what is left of the Iroquois. Inside the diner (which the menu tells us translates to "The Eatin' Place"), the specials are listed in red crayon on a bulletin board. Tomato soup and grilled cheese sandwich for $1.95. Who could resist?

Who eats here? Look around. One white man, dressed in a gray suit, green shirt, and bright purple bow tie, moves from table to table, talking to those he knows like any good politician. Another wears jeans, saddle shoes, army cap. A woman in her sixties with dyed red hair wears a Buffalo Bills sweatshirt over her white dress. Who are they in the rest of their lives?

Our waitress is a woman with short curly hair. A permanent. Has to be. In fact, all the other waitresses have short hair too, though the men behind the counter (and those who come through the door marked CIGARETTES) all have long hair in ponytails. The food is vintage 1955. Campbell's soup. Hot cheese. My grandmother's sturdy black shoes. Her apron.

Outside, there are three black-haired children, each carrying a leash, trying to let three puppies out of their pen. The dogs push open the door and spew into the road in a yipping tumble of gray fur. I catch one puppy, holding him until one of the children can hook a leash to the collar. Their mother stands on the porch above us. She does not say thank you. She does not smile.

Cattaraugus. Tuscarora. Tonawanda. On the map, these three reservations ring the city of Buffalo in space clearly delineated, set apart. On the ground, they are in the middle of nowhere. There is no distinction between here, on the outside, and there, where Sah-Da-Ko-Nee's seems to be the center of life. All I know is that one Sunday afternoon I am back in Painted Post and my grandmother Mayme has fixed a lunch of soup and sandwiches. Forty years have disappeared, swallowed by a landscape that never seems to change, for all the Wal-Marts and Kentucky Fried Chickens and aluminum siding and satellite dishes.

But everything changes. Time proves that. Long ago my father fought the Army Corps of Engineers when they decided to move the Cohocton River, give it a new bed—and then, years later, in 1972, the river reared up to prove him right. It plunged over the new highway and right down the main street, six feet of water in the old house on Hamilton—a house that had survived since 1840. It survived again, but not intact. They had to rip out the built-in bookshelves, the dining room cupboards. There stood the same blue goblets—on a new wide windowsill—sun streaming through, painting the carpet as though nothing had happened at all.

Funny, that landscape—yellow house, treed yard, hovering hills—is only external, at best a memory stilled to photograph. What lives inside, stirs and wells up in the least expected moments, is a field of wild poppies. English farmland with its dark stone walls, its green-glass fields, sky a fury of cloud. And the poppies flickering in the field. A moment of pure peace, contained, as in a bowl, though the only person in sight was myself. A loneliness so complete it felt like living more than one life.

Sometimes landscape settles inside you and makes room for nothing else. Each emotion is weighed against that inner scene to determine how it fits, whether or not it has a rightful place. Whole ranges of possibility have been discarded in the face of one flaming field.

NOW IT'S EARLY SUMMER. BLACKCAPS RIPEN IN OUR BACK-yard. I pick them in memory of my father, his careful garden. They're large and unruly, falling into the fingers without resistance but leaving a stain like a bruise. The day is brimming. Heat shimmers up from the sidewalks and nothing moves.

Easy to warp and ruin the built-in bookshelves. Harder to wash away the sound of my father's axe on a weekend afternoon. Chunk. Pause. Chunk. The growing stack of wood. His god was science—dispassionate science. He was the only person I have known whose daily vocabulary included the words *premise* and *proof.* I'm still learning how to say *was* instead of *is.* It's not yet a month since he died and he still comes to me in dreams as a voice on the phone. Sheer sound. A voice split and stacked against the cold.

The State Anatomy Board would like to express its sincerest condolences to the family and friends of Robert B. Randels and acknowledge our appreciation of the donation for the advancement of medical education and research study in Maryland. The gift of his body provides a legacy for the improved health of generations yet to come. On behalf of the Board and those medical programs, I would like to express our deepest gratitude.

He wasn't alone. the world will remember Jacqueline Kennedy Onassis. Sir Stephen Spender. Jonas Salk. Mickey Mantle. Ginger Rogers. Ginger Rogers—her fluid body, flinging itself out into a life of its own, then drawing back again, following Astaire's lead. I've read that Fred Astaire was embarrassed by his hands, his too-long fingers. Who ever looked at his hands? All we remember is the feet, the perfect synchronicity of his polished shoes, a blurred landscape of metallic motion like a hummingbird at the feeder. Who ever noticed his hands, the two middle fingers pressed down into his palm so that only the other two pointed upwards, jaunty and optimistic, objectified and oddly self-conscious in the stilled shot where the dance stops in midair?

I am left with the singular first person, poised on the brink of knowing something about myself. "Hi there," he says, his voice brightening over the thin wire that holds us up. I know the dreams will fade, the voice will lose the clear, familiar tone. Inside, poppies will stir in a breeze I've almost forgotten, spring to wiry life in blood-red fists.

I suppose we all have something we think others will notice. Something we press into the palm of secrecy. But no one ever does. No one sees the baseboards the hostess scrubbed with a toothbrush. No one looks for the crooked tooth. What worries me is the other side of that thought. What is it we think no one sees that is evident to everyone but ourselves? I touch each bitten fingernail, listen to each grumpy note of frustration. Too obvious. Maybe it's the rough soles of the bare feet I tried too late to scrub each time I went into labor. The rough sole gone deep until it is a part of personality.

In my father's eye there is a river. It bends and twists for thirteen miles until, as the crow flies, it comes to a spot only four miles from his home. In the winter, he and his friends can hitch a ride on the runner of a sleigh for those four miles, hop off, put on their skates in late afternoon light and then head back, hugging the curves of the bank on ice that glints ahead of them. I look for whatever it was he worried about, whatever he wanted to hide. But the road to his death seems so straight, so plainly marked. He signs his Living Will on recycled paper. He leaves us three thousand empty Styrofoam cups. He laughs out loud when his medical student first pulls back the sheet. "Mine has a red beard," he hears him shout.

How do you push past the imagined *fact* of your father's death? So many times he relished the moment in prospect that it seems necessary to let him relish it in reality. But in reality he will not know his medical student, will be nothing but whatever the body is without its fire.

My son William recounts an argument with his grandfather that lasted the length and duration of a thousand-mile trip—about the meaning of the phrase "metaphorical truth." My father could not comprehend a truth that did not contain the words *theorem, therefore*, and *by extension*. How would he have internalized the latest scientific vocabulary, the way physicists now postulate without expectation of final results? There are other ways of knowing. Ways the word or image drills through the surface to unfurl beneath the skin.

Look at what Plath did with what I think of as my poppies. "Little poppies, little hell flames, / Do you do no harm?" "If my mouth could marry a hurt like that!" July again on the page, but July tinged with the mad desire for the colorlessness of death. Lucky I saw the poppies before I saw the poem. It would have changed them forever.

And even Plath could see the shifting nature of metaphor, the way it is true one minute and not the next. A truth to counteract dispassionate curiosity. By October she was calling them a "love gift." "Oh my God, what am I / That these late mouths should cry open / In a forest of frost, in a dawn of cornflowers."

Does she open herself to the landscape? Does she open her landscape to us? Where does the truth reside? Sometimes I think metaphor is the magic of electricity, flick of the switch. Sometimes it's osmosis, slow seepage, transaction. July to October: daylily to marigold.

The banks of the Cohocton grew wide as the water shrank to a shallow stream. Tadpoles. Slippery, moss-covered rocks. Stepping-stones. Whole hours filled with the slow passage of water. Dragonfly wings. The way they sometimes catch the light, skittering iridescence over the convex surface. The sun hot on your shoulders. Your hair wispy in the breeze. Your feet tough. How did you finally pull yourself back from the earth, retrieve your bicycle and pedal home? And where is your mother's voice, calling you in, past the potted geraniums and the yew, up the gray steps, through the heavy front door?

Nostalgia could make of anything the perfect moment, and those moments were only the fabric of the days, ordinary and incomplete. Perfection was saved for the screen where Hollywood told us what we wanted from our lives. Provided the perfect, carbon-copy metaphor. Not that you ever felt you could dance that way—the two of them in perfect pitch, as though their minds were in tune, as though they had not practiced and practiced, behind the scenes, off screen, day after day, to reach for this illusion. They did not so much personify desire as create it. No, you never thought you were the dancer, but knew the dance could stand for something else. For what you feel when you watch the dance.

Fred Astaire looks down at his hands and they repel him. They betray his inner sense of self, reveal him to be gawky and adolescent. He puts one behind his back, or tips his hat, anything to keep people from looking at his imperfection. He presses the middle two fingers into his palm to divert the eye and create a visual deception. All he is conscious of is his hands; his feet do what they've been trained to do since childhood. His feet—they are so much a part of his interior that he never thinks to think of them. It's only his hands that flicker, tentative as dragonflies, extended between himself and the world he's always wanted.

GREEN

WHEN THE FEVER BREAKS, THE BODY REMEMBERS ITSELF, stumbles out of the forest whole and refreshed. It had been lost in the jungle, lost in the strange, impenetrable sounds of rain dripping onto the shiny, coppered sides of leaves and of loud birds shouting their epithets from hidden spaces. I imagined their colors—chartreuse, indigo, mangy peach—by the tone of their calls. I imagined them perched on some branch, just out of sight, jabbing and mocking, making mockery of everything I thought I was.

Thought you'd do something with this life you've been handed? Thought your thoughts counted in this world? Look at us, they cackle, *look at how we preen and call, unseen in the foliage, unheard even a few yards away. Thought you'd go somewhere? Don't you know your body holds your mind, that you go nowhere without it?*

So the mind spirals inward to where the body has already been. One green eye with a V of brown, flecked, freckled. From high in the maple tree, everything seems to move as though through a dream.

The father putters, planting and planting. The mother comes into the yard, shades her eyes to call upward, but I am not there. You are there, yes, in all your young fury, but I have vanished into thin air. You are memory, frozen in flesh. I have relieved myself of you, however briefly, to complete this landscape. I scan the hills you never climbed, coil myself around your fixed coordinates. The circus train in the far left corner rounds the bend, trailing its lavenders and reds, its curious displays that call out with the luster of distance. Even then, I knew enough to step back from the tarnished shoes and excess glitter.

Thought you could fly? they say. *Thought the world was a trick? That all it took was practice to make it come out right?*

Once, when my brother still had the chicken pox I'd recovered from, my father took me to his company picnic. I was wearing my red-and-white-striped overalls. My hair was in braids. I don't remember much except being there, alone, with my father, the drama of it all. There were older children playing in and out of the woods and I still remember the sounds of their names—Lanny Werner, Gail Armistead, Jocelyn LaLonde. I remember the taste of hot beans and the smell of woodsmoke and the haze of adult voices as I sat quietly at the edge of the field and watched and watched. And why is that small girl an "I," while you remain firmly locked in second person, perched in the high fork of the maple? Maybe because she did nothing but watch and, watching, became my future. Found it becoming. Found it clothed in the red-and-white sounds of the world, solitary and brotherless in the long grass, pulling the stems so carefully from their sheaths that, when she chewed at the ends, the tender shoots tasted of sorrow.

STILL LIFE WITH FLOWERS

ON THE WAY INTO THE ART GALLERY, WE FOUND A bouquet of flowers abandoned on a stone bench. They were roses—three pink roses, wrapped in cellophane—and there was a card that read plainly through the transparent wrapping "I love you forever Theresa." Lacking further clues, the story spun out of control. Did everything go well, the flowers forgotten in the lovers' rush to get to somewhere else, to be alone? Did he wait there a long time, wondering where she was, then finally leave, carefully placing the flowers where she just might see them if she ever bothered to get there? Did she arrive, nervous that he was asking too much, too soon, and did she, as gently as she possibly could, tell him that there was no chance? Did one of them—either of them—fling the flowers aside in anger? Stalk off into the fading afternoon?

Someone should have taken the flowers, enjoyed their cool spring color these gray November days. But who could have lifted them from the bench when maybe, just maybe, someone would return for them, suddenly remembered and fraught with meaning? So we—all of us who picked them up to read the card, then put them back again—walked on up the steps empty-handed. Still, Theresa remained separate from the stories we devised. She alone was real—made real by someone else's hand writing her into existence.

On my wall, my son's old half-finished painting. Table with coffee cup and sugar bowl, and on the floor a glass of pink flowers. On my bookcase, a photograph of the painting before he'd begun to scrape away the paint, to ready the canvas for something that never came later. Gone, now, the box in the upper left-hand corner, and the red teapot, green shadow that commands the center. There's a gray patch—glazed at certain angles—where something was painted and removed, now in neither photograph nor painting.

If there is light, it reaches nothing on the table, simply throws a weak shadow on the floor. Gray light of late winter, clouds dulled to pewter. Static. Even the canvas holds its breath, waiting for something to happen. Thin wash of brown paint. Gray flecks of what's missing. The mind dismantling the life, unpouring the water from the glass. Not half-finished, after all, but half-erased. A thing in the process of its unmaking.

Memory is the hidden painting. Not so much a peeling back as a rising to the surface. A reenactment. I remember roses. Yellow roses spilling from the trellis on the garage wall. The scent of roses in early June, sun-ripened roses that stayed through summer, replacing themselves as the petals scattered on the lawn. Tiny pink roses climbing my bedroom wallpaper. Ungainly, thick-thorned roses lining the walk to my apartment in Edinburgh. Dried roses, one-of-a-kind to mark special occasions. To love me forever.

Hard to put it all to rest. Heat of summer, wading in Mulholland Creek while my father looks for flat stones for his wall. Bare feet on slippery rock. The day shaken loose and singular. Wet rock, and the curdled sound of water, trickle of shade in the streambed. Wet rock, and the sun angling its rays through the pines. Home to the red-and-white-checkered tablecloth, corn from the garden, my mother's ironed sheets that insist she is at home in her home.

Some sounds sound like home. *Firth of Forth. Praia de Ipanema. Yellowstone.* But they aren't. They are simply conjunction of tongue and ear, a meeting of geographies deep inside the mind. They translate to cold windy shores, bedraggled clouds. Or devastating heat, rising in waves from the littered beach at noon. Or crowds, pushing expensive cameras past your shoulder at Old Faithful until you retreat to the western entrance where small ranches tucked under lucid sky look, from the outside, as though they would invite you in.

There is one moment, or rather, an extended moment, riding a boat on a long summer evening along the Erie Canal, somewhere east of Lyons, NY— the water stretched out silver ahead of us and herons lifting in slow motion—when time seemed, for once, to allow an extra measure of the day. On each side of the canal, trees lined the banks. And in the distance, fields of buttercups and daisies. A nineteenth-century scene, as though the canal had slowed to where it tipped backward and unrolled the highways that would supersede it. I've had the feeling before: locked in a time that made room for reflection. For a moment, I sat back satisfied in the company of family and friends, picnic already eaten and packed away, only the evening unfolding and nothing to do but let the boat return us to the dock, nothing to do but float in the stillness of birdcall and water. I remember that moment as one of the few times I knew what it was to exist in present tense.

So now I'm stuck with cliché as personal metaphor. Herons. Slow motion. But there was something in the way they seemed to hover just ahead of the boat, like shadows thrown upward, keeping pace with our pace. There was something in their long glide toward nowhere that gave purpose to purposelessness.

The mind won't stop tumbling. Isn't restlessness the luxury we bought with progress? Who had time to reflect when the work was too hard and the day was too short? So my ancestors bought my displacement with two hundred years of movement toward this moment. Voyages. Lands to be cleared. A Civil War to fight. Until at last my mother could be the first of her family to attend high school and college, could buy my twentieth-century right to be impatient.

I can't help thinking of Lewis and Clark, of what it took to keep going, trudging for days through snow in the Bitterroots, charting the uncharted territory. Using the method of dead reckoning, Clark recorded 4,162 miles, only off by forty miles in today's calculations. And Lewis sketched a total of 122 new species of animals, 178 new plants to be described for science.

The meticulous courage of science. The land a vast unpainted canvas waiting for their eyes.

After Lewis and Clark had come and gone, the Indians said, "They gave us things like solid water which were sometimes brilliant as the sun and sometimes showed us our own faces. We thought them the children of the Great Spirit." Perhaps this marks the beginning of the end. Not so much rifle and alcohol as the moment they looked into their own faces and saw there the source of the thoughts that, before then, belonged to the tribe. The singular self—though they must have had glimmers, moving reflections thrown up from water not yet stilled to glass.

On the eastward leg of the journey, one of the party—John Colter—left with a band of traders to return to the wilderness. He'd be lonely, he said, in St. Louis. Lonely without the company of his own thoughts. The self he'd discovered.

When I was fourteen, our family drove across the country to camp near Yellowstone. The Tetons in the distance and, each morning, sun stippled on water, silence distended. Colter Bay. Just one more place-name on the map—memory of people, memory of event. Behind each Cape Disappointment, each Bailey's Mistake, there's a story.

History is a succession of names. Is this the American experience? To chronicle the constant movement? Everywhere I go, I look with the eyes of an interloper. I wait for my past to catch up with me. Last night on TV, I saw the lake where my father and mother once crossed from Chile to Argentina. *Bariloche.* I have never been there, and yet it feels as though, through their eyes, I've seen that glacial blue. Seen myself in the solid water of my thoughts, untangling all the threads that brought me to this moment—now—when I deliberately reach out to touch my son's painting, my fingers feeling their way over the rough surface of the flowers to the place where absence becomes smooth and shiny.

SONORA

AND THEN THE EYE ADMITS IT SEES TOO FAR. THE mountains that flattened in the distance are suddenly there, large and purple. Or the red rock, wind-whittled, shifts from left to right. Turn on your own axis. Nothing to fasten on, or return to. The desert keeps its secrets well. Though now, on a day in early April, it seems about to burst. Orange flame at the tip of the ocotillo. And yellow haze of creosote. On the large arms of the saguaro, waiting for evening, white blossoms that will open overnight and attract the doves whose pollen-dusted wings will move again from ancient plant to ancient plant.

No matter how often I might come, this is a landscape I will never know. It resides outside the body, alien and unresolved. Georgia O'Keeffe entered the desert willingly, spun in the vortex of its heat. The colors whirled, then clarified.

But my eye hungers for pastures, small hills, lanes. Wants to be cut off from space so vast it reminds me of what is yet undone. Undoing.

Wild poppies in a field of grass: I want that day forever. Skitter of clouds. And a fleeting sense of belonging to the earth beneath me. Not this dun rigidity, resistant even to water. Flash floods cut the road in two. Then this brief blooming—and after, nothing upon nothing, unless the eye is pitched to such obstinate light.

ON RETURNING

Walking over the mud-covered little street, everything
looked so curious to me, familiar, yet not familiar. I can't
get my eyes to see things as they were to me before.
—TIM CASHMAN, letter in *Out of Ireland*

TO FIND A PLACE THAT FITS. WHERE PAST AND PRESENT
coincide. Where the landscape feels like a version of
the self. To walk out into such a place, so at home in
its vocabulary that you don't need words. Memory
eased, exonerated. The mud-covered streets of the
heart so prosaic they promise a life of their own.

IT SEEMS TO ME NOW THAT THE TOWN BEGAN AT BOSCO'S,
first store beyond High Street with its busy intersec-
tion, its red light. Wait on the curb until it's your
turn to cross. Sometimes Mr. Rosetti, the local
policeman, standing on that corner, fishing in his
pocket for coins. If we guessed the amount of
change in his pocket, we could have it all. Always,
the possibility. It begins with Tombasco's Fruit

Stand. Its oiled wood floors and Bosco himself, with his blue-and-white-striped apron, his generous laugh. The deep freezers full of Popsicles, Creamsicles, Fudgesicles. When you opened the small glass cover, cold air rose to meet you. You dipped your hand in, choosing, choosing.

On the hottest days, Popsicles were best. The others left you thirsty. Grape, with its sticky purple juices. Or lime, almost tasteless, but you could suck at the green until it turned white at the tips, granular. A nickel could buy that coldness. If there were two of you, you could break it in half, the length of its central seam, and then you'd each have a stick to lick clean—the wooden texture shriveling your tongue—a stick for something later, like poking the small bubbles of tar in the road.

Then you could wander slowly up past the post office, turn the corner at Tillman's, and make your way to the long aisles of the 5 & 10. They wouldn't let you stay long if you weren't buying something, but it was fun to look at the yarn, the darning needles and plastic cups and thumbtacks of everyday living. And we always needed chalk or a pencil or something to keep us there, up and down the aisles, including it all in our vehement desire.

Some days we went to the river. Walked along the top of the concrete dike to where it was so far above the ground we had to jump carefully down, or else turn back. Found a willow to hide under. Found a stick to whistle through the air like a whip. In my mind, that river grows into something large and impenetrable. Overgrown. Yet when I go back, I can find nothing of it in the modest stream that makes its way through the new, man-made bed.

Sometimes we saw the men from the foundry leaving at the 3:30 whistle. They spilled out over the railroad tracks with their lunchpails and visored caps. Sometimes we knew these men, but they didn't speak to us. They didn't seem to see us. We were not a part of their day.

TO GO BACK. TO SEE AGAIN. AS IT WAS BEFORE. AS IT IS NOW. Reflection in the window. Refraction. So similar that it's unsettling. Familiar, yes, so familiar. *It was there that . . . Remember when?*

TRY AS YOU WILL, YOU CANNOT QUITE RECALL THE specifics. Edinburgh, 1964. The Princes Street gardens with their burst of color. You remember the feel of it all, the way you could step from the busy sidewalks into a time that seemed to stop for a moment. The trains whistled in the station, chugged as they gathered steam. Took you back to your own childhood, when you stood waiting at the station, watching the tracks meet in the distance, then disappear. Time stops in the gardens. People sit on benches—mothers with small boys in short pants, or schoolgirls taking a shortcut, flurry of blazers and berets. Old men with canes feeding the pigeons. The castle rising above, as though the moment had existed forever, attenuating itself over the decades without deference to style or fashion.

You remember the feel of the place. The way it made you forget what had happened: the night you heard that President Kennedy had been assassinated and all of Princes Street blossomed with union jacks at half-mast. No, you felt as though the gardens could assuage it all, could encompass the dreams that rose from people drowsing in the springtime sun.

You felt the way you felt as you rose in the ancient elevator to Agnes McDonald's third-floor office at Chambers Publishing Company, where, each week, you brought her your newly edited pages of a dictionary. You began with the letter "P," progressed through "G" to "S," where you worked for months,

culling the meanings, using words in sentences, cut-
ting and pasting and typing to make a cohesive
whole. She was eighty years old, and each week Miss
McDonald would give you a cup of tea and look over
what you'd done, assign you a new letter, and then
you were gone again, out of her dusty room, down in
the latticed cage and out into the soft light of day.
Once, in winter—dusk by 3 P.M.—she showed you
the seven layers of clothing she was wearing to keep
warm, peeling back her cardigan to reveal two
blouses, a nylon slip, two undershirts (one white, one
pink), and, or so she confided since you didn't actu-
ally see it, a brassiere.

How to retrieve that feeling? I stand here after
almost thirty years, and everything has changed.
Double exposure. No more steam engines. No more
cinders to fill the wind with grit and sting your cheeks.
All the buildings have been sandblasted to a bright,
burnished hue. Even Scott's monument, no longer
stained by the soot of centuries. But the gardens are
the same. Flowers don't change. Whole beds of them,
spreading their blues and yellows and wild magentas
over the lawn. Bordering the paths with color.
Recovering the past with their perennial optimism.

AN ACT OF TURNING BACK. RECOVERY. RESTORATION. Repossession. Oh, my familiar streets. But you cannot recover what you didn't have. Maybe it's in you—a wariness that turns you inward, settles there. Flutter of hesitant wings.

ONCE I FIT MYSELF SO BRIEFLY INTO THE RHYTHMS OF County Kerry. Down into the village, past the farmer with his renegade cows, past the standing stones enclosed in their small iron fence, past the cottage where I imagined a whole new life for myself, to the pub that didn't sell any lunch and the post office that did sell tea and biscuits. Out past a golf course so vast we never saw anyone playing. The tiny back roads to Kilorglin.

The day of the Puck Fair, the way the town filled up with gypsies—signs that read SEVENTH DAUGHTER OF A SEVENTH DAUGHTER—who promised fortunes I did not want to hear. Horses tethered at each side of the street so that to walk between them was to make your way past hind legs with their threat of retaliation. Restless shifting of rumps. And the streets filling up with garbage—the discarded wrappers and cans and packets and boxes of ordinary eating piled in doorways and dumped on streetcorners. To walk was to thread your way through the trash of a day that reeked more of negligence than disregard.

I carry those crowds, pressing, oppressive, into my future, like the photo of a child to fuse with the adult he has become. I relish what I will remember. And I carry the vague and disturbing sense of being set adrift, entering a place that could not be reclaimed by merely returning. Nothing brings me to the moment when a group of young men will find a goat and hoist him high on a platform where he will be tied for three days to celebrate the way a goat once saved the town from an army in the long, long history of repression that shapes the terrible beauty of an Irish myth. Nothing in me sees more than a goat whose fate is not a crown, but three days of heat and misery with a rock band blasting below him and a wave of people pressing forward in a tidal pulse.

ONCE. THE SINGULAR. BUILT-IN NOSTALGIA. BECAUSE the eye is unchanged. So what about *never?* The perfect adverb for return, as in *I miss places I have never seen.* They hold me exactly before them, like water stilled to ice.

WHITE MOUNTAINS

SKY IS SEEN PIECEMEAL—BETWEEN CLOUDS, OR reflected in the smooth stretch of water beside the bridge. Clouds bleed their shadows over the hills, patches of dark and light that, in turn, create contour. And the hills ripple outward, row after row, in fading tones of blue until the last ones are swallowed in sky, just a hint on the horizon. Distance is vicarious, measured in sound—occasional birdcall, dogs barking up from the valley, or a truck shifting gears.

So the summer eye pulls inward, finds focus on something close. Cattails by the roadside. Lupine, lifting its purple fingers. Or the individual leaves of the lilac bush outside the door, chattering in the wind before the storm. The spider who weaves his web above the woodpile is carefully out of sight while the sun, caught for an instant on the filaments, turns what was invisible visible. What else has gone unnoticed? Sunlight is blue. Is brilliant on the mountains. Is sliced wafer thin and stacked ready for whatever season will follow. The gardener's shears chip steadily away at the afternoon—*shrnk, shrnk, shrnk*—and it is only in the imagination that the hedge behind the house takes on the shape it constantly defies. Tonight when I emerge, blinking, it will catch me by surprise with its neatness, the way it fits itself into the wide sweep of yard as though it had never resisted.

DISTANCE

IT'S THE SPACE BETWEEN US, WHICH ISN'T VERY MUCH, the width of a table. A fairly small table. Or maybe it's the space between where I thought we were and where we are, the boat drifting farther and farther from shore so that the water seems to widen, deceptively placid. At any rate, I used to think you would understand. Now I'm not so certain.

Some record players had changeable spindles so you could insert your own fat cylinder for the 45s. The spindle had a little metal catch about halfway up so that you could stack up ten or twelve records and they would drop down one by one—Gogi Grant followed by The Everly Brothers followed by Eddie Fisher followed by . . . Who was that girl who always owned the latest hits? She kept them in a red plastic carrying case. Connie Norman.

It's a far cry to the past. A whisper, but it needs to cover decades. It's a far cry to those days when I was someone else. And you were someone too, someone I don't remember. We shared nothing, so it's not surprising that you look at me the way you do. How could you be expected to know?

Sometimes the stack would grow so high it began to wobble, and the last song would swing a little off its timing, as though the record itself had had too much to drink.

Sometimes I think I can do it—describe my life so that you can actually see it. I turn off the highway and drive through the streets where I had my old paper route. There was the house with the vicious German shepherd. That one belonged to the basketball coach. And there, that's the house where Mo Newcomb grew up—the man who was a prisoner of war in Vietnam. There, I say, and there is my old house, the front steps where I sat waiting for a car to round the corner.

You would tell me different stories. Your bedroom window. The trees surrounding the porch. Your ham radio, and the rain tapping on the roof. The way you went every weekend to the city, to your grandfather's house. Yiddish.

Sometimes we simply took the whole stack and turned it over, dancing to the less-popular flip sides of everything we liked. What was the flip side of "Heartbreak Hotel"? I listened to it over and over. I listened for the moment his voice caught, dropped into an almost inarticulate mumble, then rose again in a wail of *OooohIIII'llneverknooow* before it accepted its fate with a second little catch, almost a hiccup, as he resigned himself to his own lonely voice.

I've done this before, you know. Tried to make two pasts come together. They never do. They toy with each other, twist each other around the little finger. They pretend. They pretend that if enough is said, then it will be known. It doesn't work that way. Knowing is deeper.

Sometimes we inserted a thin plastic wafer designed to fit into the hole in the record and played it, singly, on an ordinary turntable.

So let's not pretend. We cannot know more than what we've done together. And even then we see it differently. Take, for example, that time we spent in Ireland. You remember the road we walked. Well, I remember what was beyond it. What I couldn't see but knew was there.

We wore crinolines and saddle shoes, though soon we wouldn't be caught dead in anything but white bucks. We pincurled our hair. We believed in those songs. We believed in Grace Kelly, though she seemed a bit too regal to be real, and in Debbie Reynolds, though it looked quite hard to be that sweet. We believed in happily ever after, except that every once in a while someone like Tennessee Williams would remind us it didn't always happen.

Or you don't remember. When I mention a particular event, you look up, quizzical. You have no recollection. So our collective past is pulled out from under us—I have my memory, you have your photograph. They do not always coincide.

And we were fickle. We forsook Elvis for Johnny Mathis at the first sound of that smooth whiskey voice. We abandoned him for calypso, for the Kingston Trio, for whatever the music industry offered up for us to take. We were not purists. We did not complain that Elvis had abandoned his roots in the blues. We did not wish him back to the Sun label and the days when he could blend all his sources into one poor boy's only way out. We forgot him, who had not forgotten us.

Did we occupy the same spaces? Sometimes it feels oddly as though we went to the same dance, but we heard different tunes. Sometimes it feels as though time intervened so that we had the same experience, but in different years, the costumes all changed, the finger foods and the dips. Whenever your plate was filled, mine was empty.

But he didn't stay gone. He grew wider, sleazier, and we sometimes were embarrassed that we'd loved him. All those glittery sequins, those too-tight clothes. A parody of himself. The King.

Some things belong to a generation. If you miss it by a year or two, it isn't yours. You watch the movie, but you do not enter the screen. How quaint, you think—or how odd. You try it on, but it doesn't fit. Too tight in the shoulders. Not your time.

Over the years, when we'd click on the car radio and hear a song from that decade, we were the ones who knew all the words. Could hum along, from the very start. Knew it was Elvis from the first chord. Knew it was Elvis come to revive the past. Make our feet itch to step out on a cold gymnasium floor. Make our arms ache for the pure thrill of that one boy—the surly one with the black leather jacket and the grease in his hair—asking us, just once, to dance.

Do you know what I mean? Do you?

The car alive with 1957, summer dusk, fireflies in the roadside brush and an old maroon Chevy sweeping the curves of the back roads up past Mulholland Creek, the windows wound down to let in evening sound and somewhere ahead of us a hand on a breast, summer heat and the hammering heart.

Here. here's an oar. Maybe you can bring the boat closer to shore. Maybe you can reach across this table and take my hand. There. That's the town where I grew up. That's everything you need to know. That, and the time it takes to get there.

Sometimes, when there's a faint stirring in the bushes as birds settle for sleep, when the sun rests for a moment on the rim of a hill and the heat stands still before it, I think I hear that low-slung voice, thinned by time, purring away the back-road miles. It seems so far away. Or long ago. And I come face-to-face with what I have learned: our lives are a spiral and, though we circle and circle, we never quite come back to where we began.

KERRY

SO WHEN DUSK COMES, THE COTTAGE SINKS INTO IT, becomes one more fold in the hill that has held a history longer than time. Fog takes over and flattens the kitchen window light. Dulled to translucence. Paper. The mind opens it like an Advent calendar, moving inside to where night holds the four of us still, the blue cups filled with tea.

We do not belong, though it feels like belonging—steam rising from the kettle, and talk laid out like a pattern on cloth. This afternoon we stooped in the low doorway of the Gallarus Oratory, stepped inside where, for a thousand years, the prayers of monks have risen through dry cracks between stones that will not admit rain. Space without shadow. What's left is silence: the pause between prayer when they beheld the bare wall, the dirt floor, the light that was withheld. The sea reeks of darkness. You can hear it in the distance—a rustle of silk.

This is the landscape of the soul. And who would want a soul enclosed in evening? So bend again, and ease yourself out into daylight. If you can, peel back the hours to when the cottage emerged from morning mist, white on the hillside with its wings of thatch. Time is at stake. Time to undo what time has done. You can't bear its unbearable burden, its lonely churchyards, its lichen, its loss. You cannot imagine fitting these stones to each other anywhere but here, where, everywhere you turn, the land opens onto a headstrong sea.

OUT OF PLACE
Reading O'Brien and O'Brien

I. PAST TENSE

I believe that memory and the welter of memory,
packed into a single lonely and bereft moment, is
the strongest ally a person can have.

—EDNA O'BRIEN, *Mother Ireland*

EVERY MORNING, EARLY, WE WOKE TO THE SOUND OF horses' hooves—ponies, more likely, working their way up our road to Kate Kearney's Cottage. Later in the day, they would pull carts of German tourists into the Gap of Dunloe, past anywhere where anyone would have thought to build a house, on into desolation so austere it becomes an aesthetic. Stopped beside Black Lake, the visitor can still see faint traces on the treacherous hillsides where ponies (the great grandsires of "our" ponies?) carried peat on the steep diagonal down into the gap.

But in the mornings, fog still rising and a faint breeze coming through open windows reeled out into the coming day, the sound of hooves on pavement is a happy sound. There's new energy in their steps. If my mind conjures the brown-and-white-spotted horse that's become my favorite, the horse is smiling slightly as though lost in thoughts of its own. It seems to float up the hill on layers of fog with its empty cart clattering: yes, jaunty. And in the evening, when we're all walking the half mile up to the pub at the top for a night of song, the horses are coming back down again in moonlight, tired and heavy and more solidly there on the road to remind us what hours they've worked, and will work again. In moonlight, they might be coming home with the peat, pensive and utilitarian.

I first knew Ireland in the pages of books. It was lost and lonely then, as it is now. Its people worked and sang and prayed and learned to live with absence. Now they leap from postcards into life: old men perched precariously on bicycles or sitting stoically in the pubs, women with wild red hair and a trailing of babies, boys with the too-eager look of someone trapped. The Guinness lorry stops, and two wiry young men swing keg after keg into the door of the pub. A timid girl sets a plate of bacon and eggs in front of me and asks if I'd like some tea. There's a woman, around thirty, with the dark hair and creamy skin that might, once, have lifted her out of her life. My eyes take them in, then place them firmly on the pages of Joyce or Yeats, even Beckett. Only this land could cause a man to strip it all away: a perversion of lushness, stark examination of the boundary between love and loss.

So I, too, am a tourist, even if I'm living in the cottage halfway to the gap—the one with the thatched roof. When the busloads stop to snap our photos, they go home with a fake—their "typical Irish family" are actually Americans on vacation, as strange to this land as they are. But who could tell? In the town, all the sweatshirts say "Nirvana" or "Florida State" and the wearer might equally be from Kilorglin or from Prague. Kafka could be walking these streets, lonely and bereft.

⌒

Last year the IRA called a cease-fire, and Ireland has seen a boom in tourism. Visitors float over the border, circling the island and leaving money in their wake, though it's hard to imagine that the Irish, as we meet them, ever do anything but talk and smile and sing. A flat tire? "Well, God must not have wanted you to go on down that road." A ferry to catch? "Well, there will be another. Care for a pint?" A bill for lunch? Maybe it will come, but more likely you'll have to ask and then remind them what you ate, remind them you had three drinks, not the two they've charged you for.

Life lifts from the pages of books, becomes full present tense. We've already found our favorite bakery. And Ken, the brother-in-law of the man who owns our cottage, has asked us to stop by his new tearoom in Castlemaine—the one he plans to open next Friday, he thinks, if he's finished painting. He's still deciding what to call it. Already discarded: The Wild Colonial Boy, Jack Duggan's Cottage. This morning we're looking out at Macgillycuddy's Reeks—the range of mountains lifting out of early-morning fog like black paper cutouts. In sunlight, my son and his new wife look as though they belong: fixed in memory framed by oak and hawthorn or setting off in hiking shoes with a lunch of brown bread and cheese. This is the age I would have them forever, if I could write them down and leave them here.

Their wedding day was rainy. So all the plans had changed: no promise in the park with the Puget Sound sparking below, blue and billowy. When you could see it through the rain, the water was gray. Implacable. Inside, the kind of pleasant confusion you don't forget. The judge with her sure presence. All the other young men, suddenly younger. Robin's sisters and the fluster of fabric. Then my own son's heel on the glass, as though he'd sensed the tension and knew the exact pressure to exert. As though my father were there to tell the tensile strength—rather than on the other side of the continent breathing by machine, waiting for the doctors to decide to turn it off. So, for a moment, for a day, a pure joy rising through rain to remind us all that life goes on, stringing out its intricate possibilities.

And now the two of them walk out onto "our" road: a local habitation. Boiled eggs in the morning, strong tea, and Matthew's fiddle a backdrop for the music of the day. How can two weeks arch their backs and stretch, extending their claws, becoming three, then four, a lifetime, before we pack up the suitcase and rewind the clock?

⌒

In the middle of Lough Leane, we found an island: monastery, ancient tumbled stone, yew tree misshapenly shaping itself to the wall. Its branches bend and double back on themselves, as though waiting for the moon to fill them, to make of the mind an urn. How many years of growing for it to become so perfectly twisted into meaning that it expresses the thoughts of ancient monks who spent their days moving between prayer and necessity?

On one branch: a magpie, disheveled after a night on the town. How easily he moves across water—flight and return, flight and return. The stillness rises like smoke, and we know that tonight we'll have our own night—a tour of the pubs to see who's come in to play, which instruments will make their combined magic. Fiddle and pennywhistle, the plaintive harmony of love and loss. But listen closely: disturbance. Music driven from within, not completely wholesome, as though something were missing and needed to be filled. A round of pints, cigarettes, talk handed out like toffees, but the depth is in what somehow isn't said.

Irish charm, red-haired and rumpled. But at the heart of it all is something not so much inept as stubbornly imprecise: to choose is to close the number of options, to decide is to limit possibility.

But the whole land waited, expectant. Edna O'Brien knew that. In her *House of Splendid Isolation* she began in myth, in the song of a child never born to the land but longing for it all the same. She began at the beginning, with the wordless shape of the word. "It could be myself telling them to myself or it could be these murmurs that come out of the earth. The earth so old and haunted, so hungry and replete. It talks. Things past and things yet to be." Then she gives us an old woman, trapped by her own story as much as by the fugitive from the north who has taken her captive, caught in a net of violence she herself has harbored. Doomed dominion.

It's no surprise to my family that I ask them to turn off the main road, travel north through Killaloe and on, deeper and deeper into woods and narrow lanes and glimpse upon glimpse of lonely lake. We're chasing O'Brien's words now, the landscape as it pulls itself out of the page, triangulated between lake and village and market town where the man—intruder (do they call themselves soldiers?)—spent the night before he found the old woman already waiting, already wounded in ways that will let him in, ready for the strict introspection he would bring through the forced window with him. Ready, ultimately, to die for country, watching the field of vision narrow to ideology: a land of dream where all roads turn back on themselves.

On the map, the place-names tell me when to turn. In the mind's eye, there is a house where two nearly nameless people are held hostage by the past, where they find in each other a mirror image. On the page: a choice. What can be given away? An old woman waits for a moment in the mirror—the land confronting its idea of what it will become. And after the choice, nothing to listen to but the choice itself, the way it moves, inevitably, toward an orchard and a gun and something frightful and sad. And the woman? Forgotten, now, target of his calculated obsession. Forgotten, now, as the child she stole from herself rather than give it to the land. Forgotten as only the dead can be forgotten. Aids and abets—that's what she does in the end. Turns a blind eye to his violence because he loves the land she loves, or seems to. But he's from far away, wrapped in abstraction, and landscape is local, county by county, and isn't home always where you came from, not where you're heading? So he represents idea gone amok, and she is his accomplice. As simple as that.

Or, if you're Edna O'Brien, not so simple at all.

Setting her new novel in home territory, where once she drove to Killaloe to see a bridge where four boys were shot, and a new houseboat owned by an Englishman. Setting it where later I can find it in her memoir, serving up not only the source of her narrative, but also the source of her introspection:

> You are Irish you say lightly, and allocated to you are the tendencies to be wild, wanton, drunk, superstitious, unreliable, backward, toadying and prone to fits, whereas you know that in fact a whole entourage of ghosts resides in you, ghosts with whom the inner rapport is as frequent, as perplexing, as defiant as with any of the living.
>
> —*Mother Ireland*

But you are *not* Irish, you say, and you have made the word "home" a fluid state—a state of mind—wedded to feeling but not to lineament or detail, not caught in a change of season, a slant of light, or blackberries ripening at the side of the lane like lit globes of darkness. You are not trapped, like the keening fetus, in the history you would be destined to be born to. Your history does not hold you in its spell. It releases you, sends you spinning out your country's story westward toward the Pacific.

I held the map in my hand and the book in my mind. But all the while, behind us, the sea stretched bare beyond Dingle and traffic backed up behind the horse-drawn caravans. Ken's tea room, finally open, had two tables and two chairs. No name, but a sign painted by hand: THE [   ] TEA ROOM. With chalk, he fills in the possibilities, clearly leaning toward "Cooper" because a cooper once lived here. Four of us for tea. Two chairs. "Your wish is his command," says the woman from across the road, the one who's going to bake cakes when they've worked out the details.

I hold the map, but Ireland defies such strictures. Doolin is also called Fisherstreet, and without this knowledge, most of my maps are useless. And from Doolin—a town strung out along the coast of County Clare in a mile of cottages and pubs—it's not far to the Burren with its sweep of bare lime-stone pavement, close to walking on the moon. Here, the guidebook tells us, is the only place you can find Mediterranean and arctic-alpine plants growing together: the result of glaciation and retreating ice. In 375 square miles of Irish landscape, Sweden joins Greece in a profusion of color. Look closely at Robin's photograph: in the crevices between rocks, long stems topped with purple petals, and then, on the rock itself, where it seems impossible to send down roots, yellow mountain avens. One supported by the light reflected from the sea and naked limestone, the other by warm moist air from the Gulf Stream.

My father would have loved these facts, would have spent hours reading the books and then searching out the dolmens. No. I *remember* a man who would have— though in recent years he seemed to lose some of his passion for knowledge, holding instead to a passion for opinion. Opinion based on knowledge that had shifted under his feet, snatching physics out from under him. The world had changed. Yes. I feel it in myself: the desire to stop time and let the welter of memory serve as ally, as fixed companion in a moving sea. So the man I miss is a man I've partially made from memory, an amalgam of the one who taught me to chew the oily leaves of wintergreen, to make a bow-rudder in the canoe.

What he really would have loved is the pubs—the cheerful talk and the full substance of a pint. No. Again, I have to revise. He'd given up drinking on his doctor's orders, found it hard to distinguish what was being said to him from background noise. Would have grumbled, grown tired. Yes.

Why this need to retreat from full-blown nostalgia? I'm entitled. I'm allowed to miss my only father. But I want to miss *him,* not what I wanted him to be. And he kept changing, refusing to let me talk to him about his health. "I'll thank you not to meddle," not quite his last words to me. His very last were even less personal: "Remember, O.J. was framed." Grateful for the otherness of others, the wall of self that held him from his feelings. He couldn't have meant to die—too much interest in the outcome for that—couldn't have imagined what the rest of us could see coming. Or wouldn't. Which seems, somehow, more pathetic, given his tough honesty, his penchant for fact.

⌒

Fact: past tense. Locked in its pastness which is, by definition, what makes it fact. The present tense is formative. But Edna O'Brien puts the lie to that: an old woman reliving, as though her life were yet in front of her, a past so real in its remembering—its welter of memory—that it often unfolds in future tense. Past and present in tandem, opening the eyes to morning light, waking as who we were as well as who we are. And even when it's not indelible, it's there, shadow of a shadow, shaping force that leads us out into the day as the sum of what we've seen and heard. Seen and heard. Seen and heard. Broken record of event.

What would my father have thought as we slipped into the North, over the tiny back roads from Cootehill to Markethill? One of our more vehement arguments had centered on the IRA, but there was nothing: no checkpoint, no tanks. Simply a slightly better road, and then the sudden surprise of red phone booths instead of green—and shopkeepers who would not accept our punts. Market day. A cattle auction, muck and muddle. Centuries of knowledge in the raised finger, a nod, the exchange of cash for cow. But no cow in danger, no cow sprawled dead in the ditch, no stray bullets or bombs, obstinate war of no words like the man hunkered down in the closet of the woman's large house, waiting, with her, for what they each know to be a consummation. Consumed—that's what they were. Consumed, too, the writer who wrote them into being, stopping time as she held them at the top of the stairs. You close the book and blink, rubbing your eyes. Where did the hours go while you were there, caught in the house of splendid isolation?

⌒

19 April, 1995: a bomb in Oklahoma City. I saw it on the television. It was as real to me as the television makes things real. As real as Belfast. As real as Sarajevo. And later, at Lone Wolf, Oklahoma, where I met and talked with the victims—after three days and three nights of their words, it was only as real as their words. It was not red and raw inside me, but stilled to the dignity of the sentence. The period and the question mark.

Don Ferrell: "There was that feeling of guilt again. It was just like when we lost Suzy. In an instant her world ended. Her office disappeared and she and her desk, by the front window on the 8th floor of the Murrah Building, fell to the ground. . . . We never saw our beautiful child again."

Stella de la Paz: "After having made three trips into our shattered three-story building located across the street from Federal Building, I focused my attention outside on a young woman, frightened and crying, lying in the street. She was hurt, but she would live. I took her name and the name and number of the person she wanted me to call."

Allison Hatton: "As the days passed by, images of faces appeared on the screen, but these are the ones I never knew. How many times had I stood in line at the Athenian, or walked past them on the street but never knew their names?"

☙

Past tense. The whole of Ireland looks backwards, burrows back five thousand years through the narrow tunnel of the passage graves at Newgrange where light will enter on only one day of the year. Under ground. Sky without stars, but calling, calling: come back, do not forget us. Do not forget, though the vertical language on the ogham stones is not translatable, however easily it gives in to transliteration. Do not forget: we were, we have been, we were chosen, we choose.

☙

There it was—the house. Splendid in its isolation. Narrow lane, a copse, strewn fields, then back, behind two gateposts, three stories of stone. That's it. But to think that would be to think the woman real, to think her life unfolded other than on the page. Wasn't that what I thought? I was inside her head, inside her memory—an old crone brought to life by one man's furtive presence. Brought to memory as though wrestled there, pinned to the past and all it could have been if it hadn't soured at the source. Inside her internal words:

> *Once they cross that divide they're never the same again, like iron put into a fire. They cannot return to their old shape or their old ways. The saddest bit is that we're the same stock, the same faith, we speak the same tongue and yet we don't. Language to each of us is a Braille that the other cannot know. Words like justice or love or bread turned inside out or outside in.*

How does a writer go so far inside her character that she comes face to face with her mirrored self? Becomes the violence and its aftermath. Becomes consequence: "To go right into the heart of the hate and the wrong and to sup from it and to be supped." How does a writer impose a deeper voice on the intimate voice until, curled at the center, the reader listens to the chambers of the heart? Wasn't that when I knew that I knew that it could—not necessarily would, but clearly could— happen again? That our car could have rounded a curve into a whir of bullets. That other men might crouch in the ditch, waiting for nightfall. That the tongue cannot stop what it learns in the womb. Wasn't it words that opened in me the gaping windows and sheared walls and smoke of crumbled debris? "It weeps, the land does, and small wonder," but it persists. The flowers tell the story: Broomrape, Early Purple Orchid, Lady's Tresses, Bloody Cranesbill.

II. PRESENT TENSE

> *What drives me on, I realize, is a craving to force entry into another heart, to trick the tumblers of natural law, to perform miracles of knowing. It's human nature. We are fascinated, all of us, by the implacable otherness of others.*
>
> —TIM O'BRIEN, *In the Lake of the Woods*

EVERYTHING IN MY LIFE SEEMS TO ME PREDICTABLE, AS though I can find the root of all my stories in another story. Complex differential equation. So surely otherness lies also in story, and if we could only know the story, we could know the other. Surely the land holds story, as Ireland held story for centuries, as the flowers catch up the past in their names. But the flowers of my childhood were innocent sounding as buttercup and daisy, the pasture mown by the random mouths of cows, and the fields gave way to woods where, at times, we'd find trillium at the moss edge of trees or a jack-in-the-pulpit with its ribbed veins and hidden, mysterious center.

My father took us there on weekend walks. Weekdays we spent closer to home, but often George and I would slip into the field of corn behind our house, losing ourselves in the rustling rows until we could hardly see each other. Our voices lifted above the whispering tassels. Over here. Over here. I'm here.

The cornfield was where Jimmy Kilmer threatened to cut off George's ears with a pocketknife. We knew he wouldn't—couldn't—we didn't think he could, but there was the jackknife in his hand with its flicker of blades and his voice was darker and uglier than any voice we'd ever heard. My mother told us he was teasing, and he was, wasn't he? But we'd seen the way he touched his knife and the way his tongue curled at the corner of his mouth as he handled it, as though he could taste the pleasure of using it, taste our fear, and it tasted good to him. We were not surprised when, years later, Jimmy Kilmer was killed in an accident with a gun—something that could easily not have been an accident, but probably was, though he was alone in a garage with a gun at the time. Accident, because at the core of Jimmy Kilmer was something that loved living in darkness, so neither George nor I thought it was suicide: just stupidity of some sort, which didn't surprise us either.

⤙

What makes me think I can speak for my brother George more than I think I could speak for someone wholly "other"? Well, to begin with, we share a story, so he inhabits a middle ground in that shifting border between self and exterior. He is not someone to be known, he is someone known. From our earliest days—from the sandbox, the swing set, the *Jack Benny Hour* on the radio with popcorn and grape juice: until our memories fork and follow different routes. Still, to try to force entry into his heart would be to begin a losing battle. So well known, so little known, my cheerfully mysterious brother.

He was there, though, for so many events. All the candid shots: Aunt Margaret riding a tricycle on our front porch, knees to her chin as she laughed and pedaled past, the long limb of the apple tree where we inched our way out over the garden, the dusky hush of the rabbit hutch—silken fur, nervous nibbles. My father told us not to make pets. Each time there was a new litter, he told us what he'd told us before. We knew, or thought we knew. But each time my father cut the throat and hung the limp rabbit upside down from a line and then stripped the fur away until there it was—helpless and pink and utterly unrecognizable—we were surprised. And our surprise surprised him. So what does it take to know another? And when did my life diverge enough from George's so that I could imagine it without him? Could not imagine his?

Present tense: memory smeared over the surface of the day like oil on water. Something so present it is instantly there at the whim of a song, the smell of pine tar, the long hard heat of August. Present as the past is always present: warp through which the shuttle moves and moves, like someone pacing. The past performing its miracles of knowing, but the knowing is singular, aimed at the self. Local habitation—from which to extrapolate, but never from which to plumb the depths. And the more the self reveals itself, the more we know what we can never know of someone else.

So often it happens: I'm thinking of George, and he calls. We can go days, weeks, months, without talking on the phone, but when we do, time unravels. We know what the other is going to think, how the other is likely to respond. We rarely surprise each other.

When my father was dying and Matthew was getting married, I knew I could trust George to make the decisions. I never doubted that what he wanted was what I wanted—and that it, in turn, would be what my father had wanted. That was the gift George gave us: his absence at the wedding, his presence at the hospital, his unfailing ability to get things done. But how did he feel waiting alone, across the continent? How did he feel, insisting that my father would have insisted the machine be unplugged? I know he will never tell me—not in words that pretend to mean what they say.

The space between words is Tim O'Brien's domain: the places that have no words, but simply the felt sense of words forming, clay before the hand has begun to help it find its shape. In *In the Lake of the Woods,* that space widens to the territory of the footnote—what can be discovered after the fact. The mystery of another life becomes obsession. The narrator interviews everyone, looks up everything, all in service of discovering what cannot be discovered. "Evidence"—that's what O'Brien calls each of the chapters in which the narrator compiles fact

upon fact, footnote upon fact, footnote upon foot-
note: a web of evidence which is, when you take it
apart, the speculation and conjecture and imper-
fect memory and reliance on external authority
that leads to the composite.

⌒

1968: Each night on the screen, the jungle of Vietnam,
the deafening stutter of the helicopter, the faces of
my generation staring into the camera's eye. Who
were they, those young men whose eyes caught
mine? Well, we knew their names—or some of them:
Mo Newcomb, who was in the class ahead of mine,
held for five years as a prisoner of war; Don Borden,
who married my friend Kathy Sanford, then headed
for his first tour of duty. And later I met others—my
friend Jim DeCamp, who survived because he was, in
his own words, "cautious"; my friend Gerry
McCarthy, who enlisted at eighteen and now suffers
the effects of Agent Orange. Young men my age. So
why were they strangers on the screen?

Tim O'Brien tells me who they were, what they
thought, how they buried each new hurt somewhere
deep in the mind and kept on walking. How each
death pulled them closer together: a unity of fear
and dogged courage and unnatural luck. Time after

time Tim O'Brien takes me in-country, takes me inside the hearts of the boys of my generation, takes me where Don Borden went and went back and then went back again. Takes me to where they are alive inside their helplessness. "The war was aimless. No targets, no visible enemy. There was nothing to shoot back at. Men were hurt and then more men were hurt and nothing was ever gained by it."

⁓

1954: Eighth grade. Don Borden comes in from the country on the school bus each morning smelling distinctly of the cows he has just finished milking. I really did like Don Borden, had been ice-skating on the pond behind his farm, had felt comfortable in his kitchen with his mother and father. But I couldn't admit I liked Don Borden. He was from the hills, he was a hick, he wasn't "cool." So I turned my back when he headed toward me in the hall, pretended I hadn't seen him. Turned my back on the pond with its maze of paths between low shrubs that grew up through the ice, the late sun casting long shadows. Our laughter snagged on branches, lost itself in the length of afternoon held at the still point.

His story would differ from mine. He'd see a girl turn her back, pretend she didn't notice him. He'd remember the day on the pond, the way her scarf came loose in his hands and the way he couldn't keep her still as she slipped between bushes, spinning ahead of him, lost in her laughter.

O'Brien knows that every soldier carries his past into battle. And that the battle, afterwards, becomes a past he will carry into the next. So he can fashion John Wade and his wife Kathy and set them in motion around a moment as innocent as a frozen pond crazed with shadow. He can let her disappear one morning from a cottage on a northern lake and watch as her husband's life peels back to root cause, back to story. So it is not the mystery of *disappearance* that interests the reporter who is telling the story—and therefore, by extension, not *mystery* itself that interests the author. No, the author is interested in distance. The story unfolds twice removed—a mirror reflecting a mirror reflecting a mirror—to give it its odd angle of vision: its obsession buried in footnote, buried in the history of the history of violence.

Just before Don Borden left for Vietnam, George and I had an argument with him—loud party, George full of passionate intensity, our words rising over the music in small deft jabs. Looking back, we can see clearly; he was already in the Green Berets, already trained and willing—even eager. *Wrong war. Wrong reasons.* He shouted back that he was fighting for us, for his wife and baby son, for all of us. *Don't pretend you're fighting for me. I don't want that blood on my fingers.*

Righteous. That's what we were then, are now in retrospect. We fought against that war in every ineffectual way we could. I walked the streets with petitions for Eugene McCarthy; I refused to get corrective shoes for my one-year-old's flat feet (that way, he'd never have to go to this or any other war); I marched and painted signs and sighed behind the scenes. My father marched in Washington: armbands, singing. George got married and had a baby to avoid the draft.

If I look back, there is so much we didn't know as our stories were shaping themselves to fill the present. George never sees his daughter—bright, beautiful Lisa—lost to him through circumstance that sounds almost ordinary when you tell the story. Matthew is married, and complains that he'd be a better soccer player if his feet weren't so flat. He plays left wing. Who knows what happened to the signs?

What did Don Borden do over there? Three times—thirty-six months. In a footnote, Tim O'Brien confirms what we could only imagine:

> I know what happened that day. I know how it happened. I know why. It was the sunlight. It was the wickedness that soaks into your blood and slowly heats up and begins to boil. Frustration, partly. Rage, partly. The enemy was invisible. They were ghosts. They killed us with land mines and booby traps; they disappeared into the night, or into tunnels, or into the deep misted-over paddies and bamboo and elephant grass. But it went beyond that. Something more mysterious. The smell of incense, maybe. The unknown, the unknowable. The blank faces. The overwhelming otherness.

Footnote to a footnote: O'Brien turns his back. The reader is abandoned to a world of footnote but even the footnotes do not spell fact—some are pure fiction. So where is the boundary? The author is left behind: a small figure at the wrong end of the telescope. His story unwinds in the rearview mirror. My Lai unlocked and laid at my doorstep. Londonderry and Jerusalem spread out on the lawn. Did he abandon me, did I abandon him? I step out of his story and make one of my own. He was already trained: that much we know. So I see a knife, something quiet and lethal and furtive. I see the blade lift once in moonlight. Or else I see initials carved in the soft belly of a pig. A notch in the ear of a corpse. A knife prying open the lid of a can and the tongue a flickering candle at the corner of the mouth. On some dark night, Don Borden learned more about himself than most of us will ever have to know.

╭─

Distance. O'Brien's nemesis as well as his device. Fact to fend off fiction. But fact as deflection, forced exit from the self.

> We live in our own souls as in an unmapped region, a few acres of which we have cleared for our habitation; while of the nature of those nearest us we know but the boundaries that march with ours.
>
> —EDITH WHARTON[1]

╭─

[1] Another footnote to a footnote: O'Brien's footnote 70 signals that the quote is from Wharton's *The Touchstone* (1900, reprinted New York: Harper Perennial, 1991).

So the book opens spaces we don't want to know. Takes us into territory—the far north of the soul—where, given the choice, we would never take ourselves. But choice is an inner landscape. Let the dead bury the dead. My father chose his death, had written it down on recycled paper. Had signed, sealed, licked the stamp, and sent it out in rain or sleet or snow on its appointed rounds. In our hands, our father's words: under no circumstance.

No choice at My Lai or Srebrenica or Oklahoma City. And we have no choice but to remember what connects us—the past holding out its arms. Time unhinged. As though that April bomb shook loose the story of the land. The active choice of memory.

Dennis Purifoy: "What mattered was waiting for the ball to come down through the darkness, trying to hear where it might bounce off the roof. Then launching ourselves, racing around the house, avoiding the swing set and other obstacles we knew were there in the darkness. The sweet honeysuckle and the feel of the grass or driveway on our bare feet guided us."

Jack Gobin: "We could climb the gatepost, jump into space, straddle the rope and swing about half a city block out into space. There was some danger in hitting the tree, but that just added to the thrill.

Now, over forty years later, I've seen the spot, tree and post still there but rope long gone. I choose to just remember the time of the life of the rope."

Time is unhinged: so we name the place where it happened. But if the land remembers, it must taste blood. And bile. Unnatural law. And then, in 1996, the London bomb shattered the truce. Shards of metal and glass and a wail of sirens. Present tense of the present tense.

How does a writer step outside his character, set himself at such remove that if he finds a mirrored self, it is a reflection of the back of the head: a faceless, vanishing self? He fashions a man: John Wade. Unknowable, as all men are unknowable. He fashions a history: John Wade's. Knowable, in part. Collage of memory and event. He gives Wade a wife: Kathy. Herself unknowable, though god knows she tries to make connections. He lets her reel out into the darkness of uncertainty. Watches, waits in ambush, waits for what will reveal itself. Nothing. Nothing surprising. So, hidden in the first person singular of the footnote, he gives himself a storyteller—someone who has also been to Vietnam, has his own secrets, his own "trapdoors." Ghost of a ghost. Looking for John Wade is like going after Cacciato, and the end is no ending: is ended in nothing, is unfathomable, for all its foot-notes. "All secrets lead to the dark, and beyond the dark there is only maybe."

All this distance to draw a bead on the self? Yes. The maybe of the self. And no. Because there's a loose end: Kathy. Aids and abets—that's what she does. Knows all along that Wade is obsessive, is secretive, hungry for the kind of attention that can never fulfill. Knows enough to know that somewhere in that war Wade came face to face with the mirror—and that mirrors are his métier. Knows that if she looks into the look-ing glass, she'll look on through a window and see nothing but the world on the other side.

And she was not alone. Tim O'Brien was not alone. My friend Gerald McCarthy was there. The *poet* Gerald McCarthy was also there:

> And we called, called until
> there was nothing left
> except a single black wing
> hovering above a grassy place,
> and the dead were lined up—
> their names all the places
> that were us.[2]

---

[2] From "Children of the Dust" in *Shoetown* (Bristol, Indiana: The Cloverdale Library, 1992).

Name and place, inextricable. I *am* geography—
smothering hills, the contained cup of my child-
hood. And beyond them, sky. And beyond sky, the
sound of the train's passing. Lonely whine as it
screamed past the crossing, faint echo at the next,
then silence. The world outside with its held breath.

The world outside. First, my home: the village of
Painted Post, New York, where the Cohocton joined
the Tioga to form the Chemung—named for the
place where the Iroquois met to trade. To the east,
Horseheads—named for the skulls of horses found
long after Sullivan's march. To the north, Coopers
Plains—named for the trade of the people who set-
tled there. To the south, Gang Mills—lumber. And to
the west, nothing but miles of farmland and wooded
hillsides filled with Indian pipe and wintergreen.

In my father's freshly turned garden, we often
found pieces of crockery. Old toys. A rusted key, too
large for any door of the house. Nails. And only once:
an arrowhead. Dug down to something unsettling.
So we opened our fists and let the chipped flint drop
back down into the open furrow.

⌒

Chicago, 1968: crack of clubs on skulls. Dull thud.
Police. Panic. On TV, the bloodied faces of young men

shout our shame. It's in us, this war. It's in us, this violence. It's our story, over and over: Cromwell and Sullivan and Sherman and Custer and Calley and O'Brien and Borden and us.

⤛

But the land doesn't want our welter of memory, our attachment. Holds arrowhead and key in the same square foot. Sprouts green each spring. Furls and unfurls its ferns, its curious odors and textures: skunk cabbage, shale. The land doesn't listen to our stories, is unimpressed by the names we give them: love of country, justice, revenge.

Don Borden came back from his third tour of duty. He nursed his wife Kathy through her final illness: cancer of the jaw. He held her as she died. He raised his three children and put them through college. His mother still lives on the farm in the hills of Hornby. And I am the one who turned my back when a fourteen-year-old boy walked toward me. I will always be the girl who pretended she didn't know him. Aids and abets—that's what she did. Past tense of a past tense: end of story. Because I do not know Don Borden, cannot know Don Borden, am not sure I want to know Don Borden.

Once my father taught us the stars. Looking up, he'd trace a shape in the nighttime sky, give us a constellation. And a name. He'd tell us how to find it in a revolving sky—all his knowledge brought to bear on a bright spot thousands of light years away, the universe spread open.

Maybe trust is the only way of knowing—really knowing—someone else. I trusted George with the guardianship of my father's breathing/breaking off of breath. All I know is that I'm facing my own implacable otherness. Forced entry. My own heart: found wanting. History turns its back to the mirror and walks away. Even if we sit still, it recedes. And we don't sit still. We press against the future like so many moths at the screen.

CEDAR BREAKS

I KNOW I SHOULD BE HERE FOR THE ROCK FORMATIONS—
what would, the guidebook tells us, be one of the
seven wonders of the world, if it were located any-
where but here in Southern Utah. 112° heat. The car,
laboring at eleven thousand feet, is air-conditioned
cool, and I have no interest in getting out, in walking
to the edge and looking down into fathomless dis-
tance. Purple distance—mauve and violet and deep,
blood-colored maroon—two thousand feet deep and
three miles in diameter. I'd rather stop farther on, in
subalpine meadows, to lift the wildflowers from their
beds and stare into their faces. I'd rather sit on a log,
remnant of spruce or aspen, watching a stream make
its way through the grasses. A mule deer's curiosity.
I'd rather set my sights on the seeable.

We've come from Zion, which the Mormons orig-
inally named Not Zion when they found that moun-
tain men and miners had found it before them. All
that drinking and gambling and taking the name of
the Lord in vain. Not Zion, not the promised land, as

the natural spires of rock rose above them, jutting into a wide, judgmental sky.

We're headed back to Salt Lake, where water has made the desert bloom. But here, taking a break from the highway, getting a break from the heat as the temperature drops five degrees for every thousand feet we climb, we step into another time. Water's time. The time it takes to carve its way through rock, as though it has all the time in the world. And it does. We are the ones who wonder if we have the time to stop, to learn the names of flowers we've seen before, but noted only as color and shape, borders along our map of distractions. We need to know them in order to say *cinquefoil,* not daffodil, not dandelion, not buttercup.

LACRIMOSA

NOW, IN APRIL, PUSSY WILLOWS BURST LIKE TEARS ALONG the branches. Pearls of ice. The day is silver. Lost in sunlight. Lost in the shapes that sunlight makes through branches, flickering light, then dark, then light, whiplash of light splayed like fingers across the windshield.

In the hedgerows, forsythia. Whole skirts of yellow. It takes a long time to imagine each bush filling with leaves that rise and droop into a fountain, defining a space underneath, circle of shade, where a child could hide all morning in a whisper of green. It takes a lifetime to know how the seasons shift ever so slightly, what frost will do to the cherry blossoms, how one hot day will force tulips from their sleep.

This year April has been friendly, handing out favors. The sky has unraveled blue and original. The skies of a childhood, color of recollection.

᠅

When my Uncle Ray sends me the videotape of the home movie of the wedding fifty years ago, he thinks

I must have seen it before. Only in the mind's eye. Only as it unrolled before me, from my own angle of vision. Here is the confirmation I have longed for.

May 1st. Forsythia. Everything green and blooming. There I am in my pale green dress and party shoes. My pigtails bouncing in sunlight. There's George. Look at his brush cut, and fifty years later his hair is still the same. Aunt Margaret with orchids in her long, dark hair. Women—I can almost taste their names—wearing hats with feathers. The forties caught in cameo. My father in a fleeting moment, leather camera case slung over his shoulder, smoking a cigarette. Young and vital. Slim. His red curls. But where is my mother? I look for her, her absence welling in me until I panic. I know she was there, remember her there. Behind the scenes—it's her house, her party, her present to Margaret and Ray. She's the one who placed the candles on the table. I know. I was there. She was the one who ironed the tablecloth, ordered the cake, set out the gleaming rows of white china cups and saucers. I know. So where is she when the party's going, when the guests are set in flowing motion, swirling around the newly married pair? All those summery pastel dresses, and none of them her.

I watch as though I could will her onto the film, stare as people stream through the old front door, the one I entered day after day coming home from school, watch as people I can name—Martha Smith, Vivian Vogt, and the man I considered my special friend, Jack Martin, from Spencer Hill—come through the familiar doorway and down my old front steps. My father. Then me. I run and skip. We must be about to see them off, my Aunt Margaret and my new Uncle Ray, in their old gray Plymouth. About to watch them out of sight, over the railroad tracks that have long since been removed, and on up the hill toward Hornby Road and the back way to the railroad station. We must be about to wave good-bye, tangle of emotions.

Then there she is—blurred in the camera's eye, almost out of focus. You can hardly tell the color of her dress in this, the darkest, frame. Who could recognize her? Bright second of movement, bringing her to life twenty years after her death. She sweeps down the steps and away from the lens. Half a second to recognize the spring in her walk, the distinctive shape of her animation. And half a second to lose her again. I do not want to put the machine on "pause," steal her back to stillness for my sake. I let her move on out into the mutable May afternoon.

YELLOW

LATELY THE RUSH HOUR TRAFFIC BEGINS BEFORE YOU have to put your headlights on. The season's turned. I'm thinking back to summer solstice, thirty-five years ago, in Denmark. Hard to picture the elderly couple, by now most probably dead, who took us up the coast to where we could look across water and see the coast of Sweden—lined with a thousand small fires—holding darkness at bay. So why do I, now, picture the folding table they pulled from their trunk, the starched white tablecloth, the pure white porcelain cups of steaming coffee as we stirred the night away? Why do I hear the clink of spoon on saucer and the silence between us, not awkward, but the companionable silence of people who do not speak each other's language, so smile and gesture, turning inward to where words find their isolated echoes? Who could have known then that we should memorize that couple's name, their faces, the wrinkled backs of their hands, the man's slight limp as he set up the folding chairs, the woman's white hair, her pride in the silver coffeepot into which she poured the coffee from the thermos before she poured it into our cups? The next night there would be another family, another country. Soon we'd be eating fresh cherries overlooking the Rhine. And later we'd have the thrill of crossing the wall into East Berlin where two guards with machine guns would take our passports and make us spill the contents of our pockets and handbags onto the table until everyone laughed. Even that did not seem all that unusual. We were young, and summer was wearing on. I had a wedding to go to—my own—and summer school in London. Barbara Hepworth and Benjamin Britten were still in my future. Everything stretched before me, like a clean linen cloth. There was nothing to recapture then, the longest day of the year. The slow sun sinking into the sea was just another distant bonfire.

DIRECTION

JUST BEFORE MY TWENTY-FIRST BIRTHDAY, I HITCHHIKED across Europe with one of my girlfriends from college. We weren't afraid, though now I realize there were times we should have been. Like the time in Greece when, past midnight on a nearly deserted road, the two truckers told us there was something wrong with the engine and they needed us to get out so they could get the tools from under the seat. There was nothing wrong with the engine, we knew enough to know that, and so we sat still and cried and said thalassa, thalassa, thalassa, which means ocean, over and over, and pretty soon the two men got back in the truck and drove on through the night to the ferry.

But what I was thinking of was the Berlin Wall, the way we somehow ended up going through Checkpoint Charlie and found ourselves in East Berlin. I wonder what we had been thinking, can't quite recall the mood of the day, what we wanted—adventure probably—because that is lost in what happened next. We hardly saw The Wall as we passed underneath it in the underground, emerging on the other side. But it was there all right, an ordinary wall with lots of barbed wire and soldiers every few hundred yards.

No sooner were we standing there, looking up, than two young soldiers with brush cuts, maybe twenty-two or twenty-three, stopped us, asking for our passports. When we fished them out of our purses, the soldiers took them and started to walk away. Of course we followed, we weren't as naive as all that, knew we needed those passports to get home. We followed those two soldiers into a long, low building, down corridors, into a tiny room where they asked us to take everything out of our pockets and handbags, made us put everything—lipsticks, tampax, coins— on a little table. Then we were scared. More scared than in Greece. They looked so young, those soldiers, too young for the machine guns they were carrying, too young to kill and thus probably why they *could* kill. We had seen pictures of people trying to cross The Wall, people cut down in the no-man's-land between The Wall and safety.

Because we were scared, we weren't able to cry, but our faces reflected fear, mirrors of fear, and then the two soldiers began to laugh. Loud, friendly laughter. Two young men flirting with two young women. Nothing more. And then they helped us put our things back in our purses and showed us the long string of bullets on their belts and walked us back through the corridors to daylight, laughing, waving, dipping their guns in mock salute. Two young men not unlike us, now that we didn't think they could kill. But we turned back anyway, and retreated to the other side.

Odd to be remembering that day so long ago, now that everything's changed, The Wall dismantled and shipped in little graffitied sections to places like Portland, Maine, where last summer I saw a piece of it installed as a monument. Chunks of a past that contained me.

The train across Germany was old, with a steam engine, and it reminded me of childhood, waiting for my grandmother to come down the little flight of steps, the puff of steam escaping between the giant wheels. The East German landscape was drab, as though it were not late June, but early spring—grass only hinting at green, and everything dull and matted. Matte. That would be a good word for the landscape with its tiny stone houses and its clotted fields and the gunmetal sky that refused to acknowledge the sun.

Miles of it. The backsides of towns, the way trains always peel away the privacy of any place they come to.

We spent long minutes stopped at sidings, or else in the middle of what looked like nowhere. And then we spent one longer hour while the border guards inspected our passports before we could enter West Berlin. What did we think we were doing? We knew no German, except for counting to ten—something my great-grandmother Schmidt had taught me before she died. It was the only thing she taught me, since she had retreated to a childhood far narrower than my own by the time she was counting my toes in German. Still, it meant that I could order two of whatever I pointed at in the bakery window. It meant that I could count out the deutsche marks it took to buy lunch, or tickets to the horse race, where I heard the only other word I thought I recognized: *achtung,* repeated over and over, with an urgency found only at racetracks and railroad stations.

Berlin, and it rose up in its postwar tedium, stolid, and stark, and slightly soiled. Nothing was easy. Not the hotel, not the restaurant where we ate Wiener schnitzel, not the wide streets that made getting from here to there impossible. And The Wall. Although we could not see it, we could feel it everywhere.

This was not the Germany of the Rhine, with its fresh dark cherries and crenelated castles. It was not the Germany of amber beer and singing into the night. Not even the Germany of my father's reminiscences: his *gymnasium*, hiking the Black Forest, boys on their own. *This* Germany was austere, riddled with tensions, and we had no idea why it had seemed like such a good plan to go there when we were west of it, in Denmark's Tivoli Gardens, the bright swirl of children and flowers in profusion. There, for some reason, we had said *Berlin,* as though it were inside us. 1962: Kennedy still a shiny penny, and our own country far to the west, almost a dream.

In the album, my grandfather's eyes meet yours head-on, intent. 1929: he's come to Freiburg to study under Husserl; his family in tow—wife, two teenage boys, a girl. They are peripheral. He's there to think the thoughts that can only occur when you've stripped yourself of who you thought you were. When your life has changed direction. For a year, he will be German. He will come to know what it is he thinks they think. 1929: with history still before him.

There are the family stories: my father and my Uncle Willy talking into the tape. The ones about my great-great-Uncle Christ and the Civil War. In

1862, at the age of seventeen, he'd come here from Hamburg as an indentured servant, a city-bred tailor sent across the ocean to work on a farm in Ohio. It only took one kick from a mule to make him enlist. So he fought for the Union in a German-speaking regiment, two years of service that took him to Shiloh and Chicamauga in the name of a country he still couldn't quite pronounce.

He was a small man, tiny really, and so he soon was elected by his unit to camp near the rail lines, to enter the boxcars by night and toss out any food or supplies he could find. Wherever the regiment happened to be, it was his job to go to the nearest church on Sunday morning. Seeing such a thin young man, the good people of the parish would invite him back for dinner, and his ensuing stories usually meant that he returned to the regiment with leftover ham, sometimes even a pie. During battles, it was his job to drive the ammunition cart. When shells were flying hard, he would hide between the horses, praying to be delivered. The prayers were most probably in German.

"In the yam patch incident, the need for yams was more immediate than the needs of battle." Whatever that incident might be, it's gone now, no one to tell it. I have no idea what Christ did after the war, only that he was somehow related to my great-grandmother, and that he always attended reunions for veterans where he collected a new ribbon each year. I have no idea what he did because, for me, he has always been only a set of amusing stories. I have only the voices of two brothers, sometime in their mid-seventies, chuckling over his escapades. In those tales, the war recedes. There is no blood. There is only a German-speaking boy who really shouldn't be there, wouldn't be there if a mule had not kicked him in the shin, leaving a black bruise that did not fade for months. I always thought he was a Ries, but my brother tells me his last name was Wassermann.

You can't see my grandfather's eyes in the photos taken in the decade after they returned to Michigan. They are caught in shade, or averted. And then he is gone from the album, his absence a mere fact in our continued existence. I don't know which direction to take here: back to those origins in European poverty, or into the future, where my son, whose middle name is Ries, is working on the effects of light-rail travel in Seattle. I don't know how to find what it is I think I wanted.

Direction—which we think of as definitive—is relative: a relationship between two points, one with respect to the other. What leads to concrete rising under a concrete-colored sky? The barbed wire coiled, and coiled again? History is not a still life. It is made of many directions: the choice—and everything that precedes the choice, everything that follows. A coincidence of latitude. Or lineage. The seventeen-year-old in steerage; the recalcitrant mule; my grandfather's saddened eyes; two laughing men with brush cuts by The Wall.

If I went south, I'd come to a town in Brazil called Novo Friburgo. Swiss-type cottages perch on a mountainside covered with tropical growth. Huge butterflies called Blue Morphos rise up from the forest floor. Sun glints on their wings, a shimmer, and the jungle hums. Señor Weiss calls out in Portuguese. *Borboleta*. Butterfly. It is the only language he knows. He has never been to Europe; he has no idea what brought his parents here, to this anomalous spot, where the breeze gives some relief from the steamy heat of Rio. He does not know who was displaced from this place where plants grow so fast they eradicate the day before yesterday.

My sons were small. They do not remember Señor Weiss. They do not remember the words they learned for the things of their daily lives. *Borboleta* subsumed in a clatter of consonants. The stories of their great-great-great uncle have become merely a way to hear their grandfather's voice. And soon that will fade as well. We shed our pasts like skin. Yet, when pressed, my sons recall the wings of the Morpho—iridescent blue, neon in sunlight, alien even in memory.

Northwest of Milwaukee, Wisconsin, there's a town called Berlin. Caught in its name, the vestiges of—what? Someone's nostaglia? Someone's dream? An ordinary American town, the kind that might make its way into a movie, vintage 1957. There, a girl in saddle shoes walks home from school to where her mother is waiting in the kitchen. Any mother. Any girl. Soon she will leave the town, leave its tree-lined streets, its soda fountains and its hardware store, to go away to college. There she will learn to think of cities filled with wide avenues and dusky museums. She will sew a small American flag on her backpack and set off to meet a friend. London, Madrid, Salonica, Rome, Rouen, Copenhagen, Berlin, Berne. They will stick out their thumbs and hitch a ride.

THE BLASKETS

. . . for instance girls who grew up with me and went to
America years ago and made their home there, never saw
their parents since nor the Island, surely I have shared
many I may say happy years here; whatever happens on this
Island I have one gifted thing to tell you of it I was always
happy there. I was happy among sorrows on this Island.
—EIBHLÎS NÍ SHÚILLEABHÁIN, letter in 1942

ON THE FAR WEST COAST OF IRELAND, THEY STRETCH
themselves into the ocean, hankering for America.
Hunkered down. Bereft of the people who lived there.
Now they are merely rocky coast, dark presence, rising
black as the night that descends in November.

In 1840, there were one hundred fifty people on the
Great Blasket. And after the famine, only one hun-
dred remained. Still, with their fishing, they fared
better than most. At its peak, in 1916, there were thirty
houses and one hundred seventy-six people making
the island their home. By 1942, the population had
dwindled—over half of the island leaving for

Springfield, Massachusetts—and in 1953, the entire population was removed to the mainland. There had never been roads, electricity, even a shop. Three miles across water, five miles by land for a priest or a doctor. Funerals waited for good weather so the boats could cross to the cemetery at Dunquin.

So now we stand at Slea Head with nothing but the mind to travel the miles across ocean. To imagine violent seas that claimed husbands and sons from their currachs. To imagine the stony hillsides dotted with sheep, and women cutting turf for the fire. The struggle that ends in an evening of fiddle and story. A landscape of words.

DISPLACEMENT

The circle is not round.
—*Before the Rain,* directed by MILCHO MANCHEVSKI

I RETURN, AGAIN AND AGAIN, TO FIND TIME ALTERED. Something flickers like candlelight, peripheral, where shadows of shadows remind me that what I know now colors what I knew then. How many memories have I altered this way, cropped at the edges, refined and remade?

I drive past the house where I grew up just to see what color they've painted the shutters. Who could bear to walk inside, go up the wide stairs, turn left into my old room with its built-in drawers and the tiny windows tucked under the eaves? There's no trellis of yellow roses beneath those windows now, and besides, on any summer evening, it wouldn't be the voices of my playmates drifting across the lawn. Do I want to know what happened to each and every one? Better caught in midcentury amber, locked in a promise of future that takes them away from the town—diner and gas station, fruit stand, railroad tracks, Little League baseball park—into whatever awaits them. It's almost unbearable to think of how life narrows to one missed opportunity, to a house on a street in a town on a map.

Time doesn't wait. It pushes forward, surging toward a destination that, when the moment arrives, is already receding. Time doesn't hear the voices calling—"Annie Annie Over"—high and clear and innocent of the future. As the eye waits for the ball to follow, to lift above the garage roof and drop to the ground below, the names drop into memory—Billy, Jimmy, Steve, Gordie, George, Donna—while they drop off, irrevocably lost.

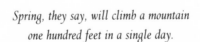

> *Spring, they say, will climb a mountain*
> *one hundred feet in a single day.*
> —VIRGINIA ELSON, *And Echoes for Direction*

ON THE MOUNTAINSIDE, IT'S EASY, WATCHING THE incremental changes, snowmelt and sunshine, the gentle tide of alpine flowers. On level ground, spring travels north at the rate of thirteen miles a day—though who knows where I heard the saying?

Driving due south, past my hometown in the Southern Tier and down through Pennsylvania, I note the town—New Buffalo—where I see forsythia in bloom. Dividing the mileage by thirteen, the answer is clear: twenty more days until spring.

Twenty days later, there it is, as though to prove them right—whoever "they" were—who must have made similar measurements in a time before odometers. Twenty days later, the past, as though I didn't know this would happen, is here, spitting in my face with its yellow fountains of gauze. Color of desire, delineation of the flowing shape of all desire, wedded to April, wedded to wanting. Buds, splitting the dormant hive, buzz at the tip ends of memory. Alive. We're alive. The increments of a lifetime, brought here, to this specific season, this welter of unbidden longing.

Where has she gone, the girl who sat on the wide front steps, waiting for the car to round the corner? Maroon Chevrolet with stuffed dice hanging from the rearview mirror. The evening closing in as she waits for the moment he will pull into the drive and whisk her away for an hour, driving the back roads into sunset, unaware of a future that will, of certainty, take them away from each other. Where is she now, so light of heart, so full of light? April arrives with its splash of color, its overwhelming undoing of everything so carefully put away. April arrives, and she slips through my fingers like a dropped coin, like dusk.

⌒

Soon the travelling artists came into a region
with no foreground, no background, no natural frame
or lines of perspective.
—JONATHAN RABAN, *Bad Land*

DRIVING THE LONG STRAIGHT ROAD FROM LINCOLN, Nebraska, to Manhattan, Kansas—straight on the map, though it has its numerous slight curves and a way of rippling like a sheet shaken out over a bed— we pass miles of wheatfields with their single lonely trees, until the uncontained sky seems to snag on the branches. Easy to lose yourself in such stretches of landscape where land itself escapes attention. The eye looks for horizon. Easy to imagine a woman simply stopping, saying she won't go on. Build the house here, where I know what I've come from, what I've left behind me. I can't go on. The imagination will not expand to take in mountains, yet another coast. This grass is sea enough and—see—that one bird dips and soars. Enough. I'll take my pleasures singly. The ground is firm. I can't go on.

She couldn't go on. She couldn't go back. What was left for her of an old life already uprooted? She'd have to make do. So now she's been recorded—she, and a hundred like her. Plow and bucket and hand-stitched quilt. Twenty-six ways to fix corn. How many meals at that one hand-hewn table? How many days with the only sound the slow turning of windmill, the steady drill of the wind? But she didn't go on. Stayed there in heaven—if that's what she called it—at least it was someplace she came to understand. Its sky revolving overhead and, under her feet, prairie, whose first impulse is defiance.

Prairie begging for clouds to form in the west and build all afternoon, a rumble, and a smell of rain that smells, if anything, like molasses, the earth sweet-sour and full of darkness. So the hawk sees only fluid grass and a line of trees along the streambed, not this parceled landscape, ruled by log and compass, these farms so square they mimic mathematics. But constant is only a "c"—ephemeral, changing, molded by circumstance.

. . . in the time that's gone.

—FLANN O'BRIEN, *at swim-two-birds*

THE TIME THAT'S GONE INHABITS A REALM OF ITS OWN. my mother opens her hands, full of foreign coins, and the woman behind the counter takes cruzeiros for the bread. In slow motion, the palm trees splay their leaves to drop deep shadows on the grass. Brazil spreads itself in hazy heat. The drumbeats build somewhere over the hill, around the corner, on a small backstreet. They fill us with their frenzy. Those hands—the ones that moved over the surface of the drum so fast that motion stilled—move now, slap, slap, sharper, faster, a flash of sound like lightning racing through the sky.

This is not dream, but memory. Time set in motion, swirling in its own vortex. This is not the work of the camera, which conjures, chronicles, allows for contemplation. This is the visceral work of the heart, palpable, ripe as the scent of jackfruit. Time so thick and solid, you can run the finger over the grain, heft and hold it to the light.

Chronology of event, superimposed on event, until the self is a coin, pressed flat, an alloy. Drop it into the slot. Along the shore, a line of men tug at their net before the storm can overtake them. They have a name for this moment—*puxada da rêde,* the pulling of the net—so it has happened before, curving arcs of history. They call to us to help and we wade through sand to find our hands on the rope, the rhythm of the sea straining through our palms as though it wanted to reclaim us.

⤢

Time does not wait.
—*Before the Rain,* directed by MILCHO MANCHEVSKI

HOUSEHOLD GOODS: almanacs, book clasps, brooms, brushes, candles, candle molds, candlesticks, china (ironstone), churns (butter), clocks and parts, combs (ivory, hard rubber), cooking kits, cooking utensils, cups, cutlery, dye (indigo), glass goblets, griddles, hearth tools, ink, lamps and parts, matches, mirrors, pen holders and points, pencils, pie plates, pots and pans, soap, spice grinders, starch, stoves and parts, tallow, teakettles, teaspoons, waffle irons, washboards, washtubs and buckets, water tumblers, whiskey glasses.

ON APRIL 1, 1865, THE RIVERBOAT *BERTRAND* HIT A SNAG AND sank in the Missouri River, about twenty-five miles north of Omaha, Nebraska. Bound for the mining towns near Fort Benton in the Montana territory, following the Missouri northward toward its source, the boat sank in only a few hours. It was rumored that there was a fortune in gold, whiskey, and quicksilver (mercury) on board. Five months earlier, on its inaugural voyage, the *Wheeling Daily Intelligencer* had described the boat as "a nice trim little steamer, neat but not gaudy, and sits upon the water like a duck." In 1968, when the remains of the *Bertrand* were discovered in an oxbow of the Missouri, two and a half miles from the river itself, not far from the DeSoto Wildlife Refuge, any gold or whiskey was long gone. Of the rumored 35,000 pounds of mercury destined for the gold mines, only nine containers (684 pounds) were found. But there was other treasure; river silt had preserved—almost in its entirety—the cargo of the *Bertrand.* Over a century later, in the dim light and controlled atmosphere of a museum, we look into the past.

> HARDWARE, TOOLS AND BUILDING SUPPLIES: anvils, auger bits, axe handles and heads, barrelcocks, bellows (forge), block and

tackle, bucksaws, carpenter's braces and
squares, doorknobs, door locks and parts,
dowels, draw knives, drill bits, files, froes
(shingle splitters), hacksaws, hammers,
hand saws, hatchets, keyhole facings, key-
hole saws, keys, lead bar stock, lead seals,
lead shot, levels, lock assemblies, mallets,
mauls, nails, nuts and bolts, oil cans, pad-
locks, pipe and fittings, pipe wrenches,
planes, powder flasks, rivets, rod hooks,
screwdrivers, screws, sharpening stones,
shot flasks, shot molds, sleighbells, spoke
shaves, steel bar stock, tacks, tape measures,
tar paper, thumb latches, tool handles,
vises, white lead, window frames.

Behind glass, row after row of shovels, hammers,
bullwhips. Tobacco. Clay pipes. Lined up in such
abundance, they are anonymous—destined for use,
but never used. Reflected in the glass, shadows of
shadows, new houses rising in the town of Hell Gate,
later changed to Missoula. Square-headed nails,
wooden screws, destined to hold the land together.
Spilled out now to show us where we came from,
what we dreamed when there was time to dream. Up
from under twenty-eight feet of topsoil, a century
preserved in mud. In the age of buzz saws, bucksaws

by the hundreds—a total of two million artifacts
that never made it into the West.

> TEXTILES, WEARING APPAREL, SEWING SUPPLIES:
> bags (woven), bandannas, beads, belts,
> blankets, bolts of wool and silk, braid, buck-
> les, burlap bags, buttons, capes, coats, dresses,
> dusters, gloves, hats, jackets, jute rolls, lace,
> leggings, muffs, needles, netting, pins, pip-
> ing, plackets, ribbons, rugs, shawls, shirts,
> shoelaces, shoes, slickers, slippers, snaps,
> snoods, socks, suits, sweatbands, sweaters,
> table cloths, tassels, thimbles, thread, ties,
> trousers, umbrella covers, underwear,
> vests, yarn.

Women. There were women in that world of saws
and anvils—women who needed thimbles and yarn,
bolts of wool. Women whose thoughts flew eastward
as they dreamed of what they didn't need—tassels
and piping and braid for Sunday best. A woman must
have been behind the urge to change the name from
Hell Gate. Who wanted to live there, when just over
the Bitter Root range, there were towns called
Eureka, Happy's Inn, and Paradise?

> FOODSTUFFS, LIQUOR, AND PATENT MEDICINES:
> ale, almonds, bitters, "Bourbon Whiskey

Cock-tail," brandy, butter, candy, catsup, cherries (brandied), cherries (canned), chowchow, cod fish, cod liver oil, coffee, cream of tartar, currants, flour, ginger, gooseberries, grain, grapes, hazelnuts, honey, horseradish, jelly, lard, lemon extract, mackerel, meat (dried and salted and pickled, mutton, beef, and pork), mustard (dried and bottled), oysters, peaches, peanuts, pecans, pepper, pickles, pineapple, prunes, sardines, schnapps, soda crackers, strawberries, sugar, syrup, tamarinds, tomatoes, wine and champagne, "Worcestershire Sauce," and yeast powder.

Hundreds, no, thousands of bottles of every size and shape, some with their contents still intact. What could the currants and flour and pecans and spices and yeast mean but a cake? Something to remind the tongue where it came from. Oysters. Faint scent of a life foregone. Worcestershire Sauce (Lea & Perrins) to take them back, and back again, to another departure, another westward voyage. Champagne to toast the new—the gold they'd find next week, next month.

Bottles, reflecting the reflections, amber, cool green, transparent. Trapped in clear glass, bubbles of time, a day caught and held in cooling liquid.

Thousands, like soldiers, lining the shelves—enough to feed an army. Enough to feed a dream.

How did they know it was the *Bertrand?* A child's slate, with the name Fannie burned into its wooden frame, found among the possessions of a family. And a list of passengers, showing a Fannie Campbell, daughter of J.B. Campbell, who had settled earlier in Gallatin.

But the shoes . . . Most "mass produced," made on lasts designed to be worn on either foot, three thousand leather boots and shoes wait for an owner. Men's and women's. Children's. Baby shoes. These are not the poignant reminders of human loss— run-down heels, leather shaped to living bone—not time that was, but the unworn shoes of the time that might have been.

⌒

I want to take the rain to heart, let it move like possibility,
the idea of change.
—KATHLEEN NORRIS, *Dakota*

FROM GRAND FORKS, NORTH DAKOTA, THE RED RIVER flows north into Manitoba. The experts are at work, sounding the depths—a calculus of water. They predict the crest, the path of destruction as the floodwaters move toward Winnipeg. Meanwhile, whole cities are locked in water. Knee-deep in silt.

Where did I hear it, that only four major rivers in the world flow north? The Nile, of course. But where are the others? What determines "major"—the size of the river? The importance of the country? Then or now? The Elbe, though it turns west in order to reach the Baltic. There are several in Russia, though on the map they look small, no cities to hold them in place. The Lena is huge, but that's in the middle of Siberia—I imagine it locked in arctic ice, no use to anyone. The Garonne, moving down from the Pyrenees into wine country? Something in Turkey? Maybe Australia, though they're mostly east or west. Not much in China. Does the St. Lawrence count? There's the Mackenzie, for sure, named for the man whose overland trek across Canada led him to the Pacific in 1793, twelve years before Lewis and Clark.

I live near a river that flows due north. The Genesee rises in the foothills of the Alleghenies, cuts its way through the Letchworth Gorge, then makes a beeline for Lake Ontario, and, in the end, the St. Lawrence and the Atlantic. Now, from my television, I've learned of another—the Red, whose full name is Red River of the North—all too real as it forces its way across borders. Four days downriver (up-map), we already know what will happen. A sugar factory in Manitoba with thirty million dollars worth of sugar to save. Where does sugar go in a flood?

⌒

The body is a naïf: among the tenses, it knows only the present.
—DENIS DONOGHUE, *Warrenpoint*

RIO IS A BODY OF SOUND. THE CANARY SINGS OF SPIDERS on the beach. *Itaipu. Itaipu.* The song is caught in a web. The windows roll out to let in the light—late light that sighs, then disappears in an instant of dusk. Light to dark, just like that. Equatorial light, and equatorial darkness. When it rains at night, the rain falls straight and hard, plinking the shutters. Rafters of rain. In the morning, there's a steady drip from the jungle leaves. Drip to the patio. Drip again. And then silence, as the sun burns through the palms.

My mother rises in Rio, caught in a language that will not cross water. She lives inside the sounds of her childhood. How far she has come from the flat farm in Michigan. How can she be expected to twist her tongue around the nasal vowels, the syncopated beat of Portuguese? She opens her hands, full of money. Take, her eyes implore. Take what it costs.

She was a woman who walked five miles to school. Worked her way through high school, living in town, taking care of other people's children. Worked her way through college, waiting on tables. Work was her life. And here she is, alive again, in the land of play, in the present tense of reactivated dream, streets strewn with color, elaborate rivers of yellow and blue. And all the while the hot sun of January simmers in the sky.

> *If Hell lay to the west, Americans would cross*
> *Heaven to get there.*
> —ANONYMOUS, National Homestead Museum,
> near Beatrice, Nebraska

IN MEMORY, WE STAND IN A PARK ABOVE THE COLUMBIA River on the far west coast of Washington State. Carved into a large pine—"William Clark December 3rd, 1805. By Land from the U. States in 1804 & 1805." They had come from somewhere else, up the Missouri on a barge, then by canoe, over the Rockies on horses bought from the Shoshones, guided by friendly Nez Percés down the Columbia to where, on

November 7, 1805, they first sighted the Pacific. "Great joy in camp we are in *view* of the *Ocian.*"

But it wasn't the ocean, and it took over a week to find the real thing. Nothing was as they had imagined it. Everything was gray—the cliffs, the water, the sky itself. Winter was coming. They held a vote and set up camp across the river in what is now Oregon, in a place they named Fort Clatsop after the neighboring tribe.

"Rained all the after part of last night, rain continues this morning."

"A cool wet raney morning."

"A cloudy foggey morning Some rain."

At the end of the winter, Clark noted there had been only twelve days without rain, and only six with sunshine. Clark—with his bias for numbers, charts, maps—counting off the days, measuring the miles.

Meriwether Lewis is more introspective, more inclined to observe the ways of those Indians who had, until now, been unknown to white men: "I told these people that I had come a great way from the East up the large river which runs towards the rising sun, that I had been to the great waters where the sun sets and had seen a great many nations all of whom I had invited to come and trade with me on the rivers on this side of the mountains, that I had found most of them at war with their neighbours and had succeeded in restoring peace among them, that I was now on my way home and had left my party at the falls of the missouri with orders to decend that river to the entrance of Maria's river and there wait my arrival and that I had come in surch of them in order to prevail on them to be at peace with their neighbours particularly those on the West side of the mountains and to engage them to come and trade with me when the establishment is made at the entrance of this river to all which they readily gave their assent and declared it to be their wish to be at peace with the Tushepahs whom they said had killed a number of their relations lately and pointed to several of those present who had cut their hair as an evidence of the truth of what they had asserted."

Lewis had promised President Jefferson that he would prepare his journals for publication, but he hadn't touched them when he committed suicide in 1809. In 1815, a narrative account of the expedition was published by Nicholas Biddle of Philadelphia. Then nothing until, in 1904, a limited eight-volume set, edited by Reuben Gold Thwaites of the Wisconsin

State Historical Society, was printed. The journals were not widely available to the public until 1953 when Bernard DeVoto edited and published *The Journals of Lewis and Clark.* One hundred and fifty years for history to surface.

In *The Americans,* Daniel J. Boorstin notes: "Striking evidence of the American need for new expressions was the many English words which the Lewis and Clark party were now using with new meanings. These included: baggage, bar, barren, biscuit, bluff, boil (n.), brand, brush, buffalo, bug, chance, chunk, clever, corn, crabapple, cranberry, creek, crow, cuckoo, dollar, Dutch, elder, elk, elm, fir, fork, gang, gap, glade, gnat, grouse, hazel, hornet, hound, hump, knob, lick (n.), lodge, lynx, mad, make out, mammoth, meal, medicine, mink, mistletoe, notion, onion, otter, pantaloon, partridge, pattern, pelican, pheasant, plunder, police, quail, raft, rat, rattle, raven, roasting ear, rock, run (n.), rush, salmon, scalp (v.), settlement, sick, sign, slash, snag (v.), snipe, some, split (n.), stage, store, stud, suit, turkey, twist, village, whip, woodsman."

Sassafras, butte, tomahawk. Prairie-dog, mule deer, service-berry. New words to send back east. *Snag* (v.), recorded but inaccessible by the time the *Bertrand* begins its journey.

⁓

Time moves not forward, I think, but round and round and round
until, when the heart is involved, there is no now or then . . .
— LEE K. ABBOTT, *"Here in Time and Not"*

IN THE TIME THAT WILL BE, THERE ARE ENDLESS alternatives. Dream flows to dream. The girl with her heart full of waiting is there, circling and circling in search of herself. And the woman who knows that what cannot be cannot be, decides, for an instant, it can. She tries on the lover she would have been if she could, tries her on and finds her to her liking. The time that will be is not caught up in detail, snagged on the roothairs of remembered event. It does not play itself over and over in the mind, revolving on its turnstile of hurt. Its roundness is a snail's shell, spiraling inward, to where the mind is a filament. In that time, the floods recede. The soil lifts itself from the sunken steamer and it chugs into the twentieth century, full of hope and whiskey.

The neighbors' daughter skips down the sidewalk. Her sneakers make the shuffle, the shift of weight onto the other foot, the little leap, with such ease. Her breasts are nubbins under her sweater. Everything budding. She skips into her place in the world.

In the time that will be, all rivers flow north.

Nothing will be caught in centuries of stone. Time is cast in future tense, spinning at the center of desire. Always April. Always before the rain. It does not carry the weight of words, their accumulated baggage, their inflection and nuance that makes for what was, what will always have been.

⤲

Five centuries of blood . . .
—*Before the Rain*, directed by MILCHO MANCHEVSKI

THE PHOTOGRAPHER RETURNS TO HIS LAND. HIS LOVER cannot call, cannot make her voice carry over fragile wires into an ear that won't admit her sounds. She stands at the edge of space. Two small boys notice the Englishwoman who does not belong, is not of this place, this time. She has come here—where the land is timeless—before the violent events that would bring her here have occurred. She is a presence, as old as the hills. Her child will inherit this landscape. This welcome rain that washes the slate of history.

You are the photographer returning to his village in Macedonia. In the movie, it takes a minute for your cousin to recognize you and, in the end, the others think of you as "not being from here." But you are from here—from there—because there's nowhere else to be from but where you're from, before the world imposes the world. The hills surround you. Smother and smolder and stoke the fires of discontent.

The photographer moves toward the moment he's already photographed. He has come back to Macedonia because he has been a part of the violence he wanted to prevent. He has come home—to violence yet to unfold. Soon he will act, and his action—all present tense—will not be enough to bridge the gaps in the fallen world. Words have failed. His pictures have failed. And you can see it on their faces—all of them—that nothing will stop what's about to happen. The priest waits for rain, thunder in the far valley. What does god wait for? Nothing. He is timeless. He has no hindsight, no vantage from which to discover cause and effect. And if he has foresight, it is heartless, is governed by an I-told-you-so that smacks of predestination. The photographer's lens stops time, but he has stopped his lens. He has put down his weapon and walks upon the old old earth.

My own background was presented to me as almost history-free.
———CHARLES FORAN, *The Last House of Ulster*

WE SEE IT HAPPENING BEFORE OUR EYES. TRANSLATED on the screen, the written words leap out at us. And on our television set, the war begins, plays itself out in its myriad senseless fashions. What is one mountain? Another?

Ask the Albanian girl in the movie. Ask the Irish Catholic in Warrenpoint. If you grow up there, you know the differences. Unsaid and unsayable. You know which shop to frequent, which farmer's friendly. You know where you came from—each stone has its story—and where you are going. You're going nowhere, not out of here, where even the mountains dress themselves in mourning. And so the dream hardens to chalky stillness. You identify yourself. You are home.

If it is going to rain, it will rain the cold, spiraling rain of the seacoast. Blinding rain that will wash in from the sea in a shroud of fog. The day will close down. The streets will be dark with the words of the sea, dark with the blood that is yet to be shed in a time that surely will be.

. . . and to measure it
continuously
—JONATHAN HOLDEN, *Ur-Math*

EVEN FOR THOSE OF US WHO ARE GODLESS, THERE comes a moment of sheer faith. For me, it was when I realized that Δx had become dx—not an approximation, but the thing itself. I'd moved my thinking ever closer to that moment of belief. And then the world opened. At my fingertips, the power to answer the questions that lie beyond questioning, an internal calculus, measuring the self against the rate of change in the self, or against the rate of change in the world. The only constant, the unredeemed past.

The gray stone walls climb the hills as if they are part of the landscape, a natural order imposed by nature for man's convenience. The Yorkshire countryside reels under the clamor of the Sunday bells— a rift in the sky, sound pouring through like molten glass. REDEEMING THE TIME—those are the words on the church tower. But time does not wait. It's the past that needs redemption, and the past is locked away, moving in the time that's gone.

The bells are gone, sounding now in memory, no, a memory of a memory of bells. It's easier to bring back image. I see myself standing in a field of poppies, wind in my hair, and think of the way the sound rose, as if on wings, from the valley below. Unseen bells, so even then their circular motion, and the hands pulling full force at the ropes, had to be imagined. And now I stand mute, in a field of flowing red, straining my ears for that dissonant scale, ringing the changes, counting the intervals between notes, the intervals of silence into which the moment will slip of its own free will.

⌒

It was as if I were seeking the nature of a verb which had no infinitive, only tense and mode.
— ROLAND BARTHES, *Camera Lucida*

HIGH OVER THE GARAGE ROOF, THE SOUND OF CHILDREN'S voices—"Annie Annie Over." What if the ball never appeared? Left us hanging there, breathless, waiting for the universe to fall back into order? What if constant was never "c," but something fixed and irrevocable? What if my life had found its simple closure and I'd settled there, planted my garden, waited out winter with its high-pitched whine? The spring would find me frozen in place. Time would have gone on, spiraling higher and higher, with the vantage of height, looking down on the landscape until it flattened to the equivalent of prairie, all topology lost in another kind of detail, the residue of a thousand lives superimposed on one square foot. If geologists cut through the rock, they'd find evidence of each of us, straining against a wind that carries those voices back to their source, and the ball dropping back to the hand that tossed it, and, before that, to the silence that precedes the words, and, before that, to the land itself, mute and indecipherable.

BAHIA DE TODOS OS SANTOS

WHITE.   White is the color of faith. Of salvation. In
         Salvador, women spread their white skirts
         as they sit on the corners, cooking vatapá
         or selling beads. Their heads are wound in
         gleaming bandannas to stave off the relent-
         less sun. White upon white. And the
         bleached steps to the churches are crested
         with women, flowers that rise into the air
         like flaming birds.

FLAMES. The beach is a forest of flame. Each candle
         held in a cup of sand. At midnight, the
         women walk backwards into the ocean.
         When they return, dropping onto the sand,
         dripping and bedraggled, they have left
         behind their boats of fire. On each boat, a mir-
         ror; in each mirror, a candle; and in the water,
         a million reflections. Fluid, watery light.

WATER.   We filter it first through a tall terra-cotta
         urn, then boil it for drinking. We wash our

vegetables in boiled water. Strange, exotic vegetables, especially xuxú, chartreuse, lit globe in the vendor's hands. And rich, red-seeded passion fruit with its musky taste—maracujá. The word rolls around the mouth like a marble. Nightsong.

NIGHT. The sound of things on the edge. Jackfruit drops from the trees in the garden next door. Over the tiled roofs, someone calls in a throaty voice. Sometimes a dog. Or traffic on the main boulevard. More often, though, there is an indiscernible hum just underneath the other sounds, something waiting to grow large, something wanting translation.

WANT. In the market there are hands inside hands, asking for coins. The man with no legs scoots on his makeshift cart. Children thrust even smaller children into our faces. Their teeth are shattered. They rap on the windows for money. They won't go away. And you—you want too, so you scatter some change and retreat.

CHANGE. Nothing changes. The language circles you like a vulture. Unfamiliar, except in the way you now know you will always feel strange in its presence. Noon. The light is so intense that colors spin and give off sparks, like glints of sun on a swimming pool. In the depth of shade, shadows go green and leisurely. They belong to another time, or so it seems.

TIME.   It climbs the sky and floats there, hazy and unredeemed. Measured in a foreign tongue. Time erupts like a hive, itching the palms, the inner thighs. It flows like a river in January where tropical water has never been stilled to the bone. The sun hesitates, then drops in an instant into the sea, leaving its afterimage.

AFTER.   Everything is a dream you might have lived. The words go distant and cold. Flags are furled and dancers spin counterclockwise on the reel of memory. Once you sang about the quarrel between the clove and the rose. Equatorial songs, bred of abstraction. Now you live in a land of detail. Grass is the softest of greens, and snow is unutterably white.

REVOLUTION IN THE RAIN

I seem to be falling in love with the world.
And something in me is afraid.
—P.K. PAGE, *Brazilian Journal*

I ARRIVED IN RIO DE JANEIRO IN 1971, FRESH FROM THE America of the Civil Rights Movement, fresh from our protests over the war in Vietnam. I arrived knowing I would live under a dictatorship, though it was hard to tell that it was a dictatorship. There were soldiers, yes, but only a few. And the people danced in the streets. There was music. Heat is what I remember. Heat, and the color green.

1951: ELIZABETH BISHOP STANDS NEAR THE STERN, staring into black water where the froth from the wake cuts it in little white circular eddies. Land comes into sight, first a dark blue and then studded with white. She looks back into the water, searching its blackness. When she looks up again, everything is close—the white magic on the hillsides defines itself as shed, oil tank, half-broken fence. Santos. The world reconfigured, no longer imaginary, but real: "is this how your country is going to answer you // and your immodest demands for a different world?"

THERE ARE TENSIONS IN BISHOP'S POEMS, TENSIONS between what is stated and what is implied.

BRAZIL, JANUARY 1, 1502

Januaries, Nature greets our eyes
exactly as she must have greeted theirs:
every square inch filling in with foliage—

and the jungle grows up before us in precise, anatomical language. The leaves—blue, blue-green, and olive—give way to flowers. Her reticence is both her weakness and her strength.

IN 1959, P.K. PAGE, WIFE OF THE CANADIAN AMBASSADOR to Brazil, herself a poet, wrote in her journal: "But we did have one eventful night when we wakened by what I thought were pistol shots ringing out in the garden. Silence. Then they rang out a second time. As no voices were raised and there was no further noise, we presumed the revolution had not really begun."

THE COUNTRY SEDUCED ME WITH HEARTS OF PALM AND fragrant bananas. With rosewood carvings and tiny blue-tiled tables. Delicate concrete bridges that seemed to float on air. The beat of the samba, like the accelerated heart of desire, pulsed under everything. Green, everywhere green. The country claimed me, and I was caught in its undertow.

1961: IN HER PHOTOGRAPH, THE CAMERA TILTS AS though the ship itself were tipping. Dizzy. The horizon at an angle. Wide, white water. Sheds on stilts. The busy dock, teeming with people, umbrellas. Two men in straw hats carrying a large package over a narrow gangplank. And in the far top right, passengers on the ship leaning out to watch, giving us our vantage point. The Amazon at last. We know she's there, behind the lens. Observant. Observing. Choosing the adjective. She imagines the world. Removes it from politics or poverty. Removes it from time.

Like a photograph, "Santarém" catches her there, innocent in her newness:

That golden evening I really wanted to go no farther;
more than anything else I wanted to stay awhile
in that conflux of two great rivers, Tapajós, Amazon,
grandly, silently flowing, flowing east.

Suddenly there'd been houses, people, and lots of mongrel
riverboats skittering back and forth
under a sky of gorgeous, under-lit clouds,
with everything gilded, burnished along one side,
and everything bright, cheerful, casual—or so it looked.

"Or so it looked." Four words to turn the poem.
Those accurate adjectives, the way they shift in their
kaleidoscope until they not only describe place, but
emotion, defining the edges on which she lived.

BISHOP'S *TIME/LIFE* BOOK, *BRAZIL,* COVERS ALL THE THINGS
such a book should contain—demographics, history,
politics, art, architecture, religion, sociology,
sports. Written in 1962, published in 1963, its politics
are bland, almost an apologia. Bishop is more
interested in the legendary Tiradentes, Brazil's
failed revolutionary, than in the forces at work in
the present that are leading to the inevitable: the
dictatorship of 1964. The one that would last for
twenty-one years.

> Even the hillside favelas of Rio and other
> cities have a delicate if melancholy beauty.
> Built of old boards, tin cans, bamboo, sacks
> or any other material at hand, they are light
> and graceful, piled up against the slopes like

> birds, nests, painted in faded colors and fes-
> tooned with steps, ladders, potted plants
> and bird cages.

Her portrait may be accurate, but it fails to convey the very poverty she has documented. Language not only bridges the gulf, it estranges as well. She sees and describes with a stranger's heightened awareness.

P.K. PAGE SAID IT MORE OPENLY:

> We drove today up over the hills and through
> the favela, which should make any sensitive,
> decent person devote his life to social reform,
> but I'm afraid my initial reaction was one of
> fierce pleasure in its beauty. Turning a corner
> we saw a group of vividly dressed people
> standing against a great fortress of square
> gasoline tins painted every conceivable colour.
> Water, of course. And socially distressing.
>
> But my eye operates separately from my
> heart or head or in advance of them and I
> saw, first, the beauty.

154 :: JUDITH KITCHEN

LATER, I BECAME AFRAID. OF ELEVATORS THAT SUDDENLY plunged three stories to the ground. Of the news each night—the number of deaths by drowning, by dehydration. Of amoebas in the water, ubiquitous beggars, taxi drivers speeding through red lights. And of fires in high-rise apartment buildings, innocent walls with their hastily spraypainted slogans. Of how it didn't seem as though I ought to be afraid.

WE'VE ALL SEEN IT. THE PHOTO OF ROBERT LOWELL AND Elizabeth Bishop sitting on the beach at Copacabana. Lowell is young, unruly. Black shirt, white shorts, black socks and shoes. Bishop is more indeterminate, demure in her dark skirt, her printed blouse, her sunglasses. Around them, bird kites strain against the wind, tethered to sand. One large white wing, covered with black spots, nearly swallows Bishop. She seems so tiny beside it. Lowell is more dominant, but he, too, pales beside their latent energy. Black on white, circle within circle, the kites become a flock. Behind them more, then more, until they merge with the umbrellas, black stripes on white disks, the beach a composition of flight. Lowell seems about to take off, while Bishop anchors herself, solidly there behind the dark lenses that keep us from seeing her eyes.

But if the streams and clouds keep travelling, travelling,
the mountains look like the hulls of capsized ships,
slime-hung and barnacled.

The scene slips by, as though she had not been the
one to slip away, back to the dream of the barnacle-
covered mermaid that she had once recounted to
Lowell. The one he had repeated in his poem for her.
"Remember?" he asked. How could she not remem-
ber? Her past stood out in bas relief.

APRIL 1964, BISHOP WROTE A LETTER TO HER FRIEND,
Dr. Amy Baumann:

> A few brave generals and the governors of
> the three most important states got together,
> and after a pretty bad forty-eight hours, all
> was over. Lota was very brave—or else
> extremely curious. The originally scheduled
> anti-Communist parade turned into a vic-
> tory parade—more than a million people in
> the pouring rain. It was quite spontaneous
> and they couldn't *all* have been the rich
> reactionary right!

AT THE COCKTAIL PARTIES OR THE POOLSIDE, CONVER-
sation was bright, strained, superficial. We laughed
out loud in aromatic air. We did not talk politics,
though everyone knew a story. I knew one myself:
our friend from New Zealand's car, somehow strayed
onto the wrong road late one night, the whine of
bullets. In the morning light, the bullet-riddled pas-
senger door made him think he'd been lucky. His
consulate registered a complaint, and that was the
end of it.

IN MAY OF 1964, LOWELL WROTE TO BISHOP:

> I have a vague image of a sequence of poems
> through which the Revolution moves—no
> obvious argument or polemic, but the thing
> embodied, there in all its awfulness, absurd-
> ity—good, bad, real, confused, clarified, in
> the end judged. I don't mean anything neu-
> tral or beyond politics. Rather the opposite,
> everything rescued from the giddy, hard
> superficial clichés that the removed give
> realities, that we all give even what we know
> well. I am thinking really that the
> Revolution might give a thread for you to
> draw together the gathering impressions of
> your ten years' stay.

But she couldn't do that. She could only respond that it was "a nice quick revolution in the rain." She was caught up in the colors of her exile, mesmerized and charmed in her exile. And it was fear of exile that kept her in exile. It would have taken a different person, with different interests. Someone who, like Lowell, was willing to mine the personal, was willing to act on his beliefs, go to jail, go anywhere he wouldn't have to face his manic demons. It would have taken a different person, one who had no demons of her own.

FOR OVER TWENTY YEARS, BISHOP HAS HER OWN, PRIVATE Brazil. Lota, and their house in Ouro Prêto, their apartment in Rio. She looks out at the colors—the fiery chaos of color—and she sees clearly in black and white. Her childhood comes into focus. Her intense and lonely childhood. The poems flow. Like water in the streams of this new country. Like the parade of people on the streets of Copacabana. Like the insistent twang of the berimbau, its one string plucked and plucked again, resonating through the coconut shell until it is muted on the belly, language stifled in the gut. Bishop goes back to the white-washed cottage in Nova Scotia, to the waiting room where she discovers a self. An Elizabeth, she calls her. That named center of our being. That self-inflicted wound through which we negotiate the world.

http://www.desaparecidos.org/brazil/victimas/listas

LISTADO DE DESAPARECIDOS EN BRAZIL
List of the Disappeared in Brazil
Archdiocese of São Paulo, 1986
Torture in Brazil, appendix iii

1. Adriano Fonseca Fernandes Filho   -1973 [A]*
2. Aluizio Paihano Pedreira Ferreira   -1971
3. Ana Rosa Kucinski Silva   -1974
4. André Crabois   -1973 [A]
5. Antônio "Alfaiate"   -1974 [A]
6. Antônio Alfredo Campos   -1973 [A]
7. Antônio Carlos Monteiro Teixeria   -1972 [A]
8. Antônio Guilherma Ribeiro Ribas   -1973 [A]
9. Antônio Joaquim Machado   -1971
10. Antônio de Pádua Costa   -1974 [A]
11. Antônio Teodoro de Castro   -1973 [A]
12. Arildo Valadão   -1973 [A]
13. Armando Teizeira Frutuoso   -1975
14. Áurea Eliza Pereira Valadão   -1974 [A]

15. Ayrton Adalberto Mortati   -1971
16. Bergson Gurjão de Farias   -1972 [A]
17. Caiuby Alves de Castro   -1973
18. Carlos Alberto Soares de Freitas   -1971
19. Celso Gilberto de Oliveira   -1970
20. Cilon da Cunha Brun   -1973 [A]
21. Ciro Flávio Oliveira Salazar   -1972
22. Denis Antônio Casemiro   -1971 . . .

*The list contains 125 people in all, in alphabetical order by first name.
[A] indicates those who died in the "Araguaia Guerrilla" movement.

WHEN I LEFT, I TOOK WITH ME THE SONGS SUNG BY
Natalia as she washed our clothes. I took the taste of
black beans and the indelible scent of uncertainty. I
took my children and fled because I did not know
what it was that I did not know. *Marcha soldado, cabeça de
papel, si não marcha direito, vai prisão no quartel:* march soldier
march, in your paper hat, if you don't march correctly,
you'll be a prisoner in your room.

WE ALL HAVE OUR OWN, PRIVATE BRAZIL. THE PLACE OF
the heart. The place we absolve of judgment because
to judge would be to sacrifice the heart. It holds us to
ourselves in ways we do not want to understand. Its

colors are ivory, indigo, mauve—the muted shades, the subtle mixes. Olive and lime and chartreuse. Green, everywhere green. What we leave unsaid is nevertheless articulated. Is gesture. Is golden evening, opening itself to our own immodest demands.

WHITE

THIS AFTERNOON VENETIAN BLINDS LET IN THEIR
ladders of light, blurred at the edges, bleached, like
the land itself, covered in snow, the trees blown
ragged and restless. Stray branches snap in the wind
and scud across the yard. Everything else is on hold.
Evening comes early, filling the window. On the wall,
the painting holds a field of snow, a cluster of build-
ings huddled under two pines—the blacks and
whites of my son's twentieth year. The scene is so real
it holds the restless light exactly as though the inter-
vening years were simply a border across which I
might enter his lonely room, look through his win-
dow toward snow-covered hills that rise in latent
strips between the blinds.

DISTANCE AND DIRECTION

> *Even today*
> *you can hit them and pinch them*
> *and kick them. You can shake them,*
> *scream into their ears. You can cry.*
> *You can kiss them and whisper and moan,*
> *smooth their combed and parted hair, touch*
> *the lips that yesterday spoke, beseech,*
> *entreat with your finest entreaty.*
> *Still, they stare without deviation,*
> *straight into distance and direction.*
>
> —PATTIANN ROGERS,
> *"The Dead Never Fight Against Anything"*

THERE'S THE ANGER, YES, THAT HE WOULDN'T LISTEN.
Though he was eighty-three, nearly eighty-four, and
still in possession of every single faculty. So why
wouldn't he listen to me, who had only his best inter-
ests at heart? Why resist the daughter who had come
to Baltimore after his first operation, had cried and
moaned when she saw him delirious and drugged in

intensive care, his chest torn open and stapled shut again? Cried and moaned that this was unfair, that it was inhuman to make someone suffer this way.

And then he began to mend. To walk down the corridor. To return home. To slowly manage the seven steps up to his apartment. To spend time with the doorman. To walk around the block. To take his small cart the two blocks for groceries. To take the bus across town.

And so she saw that medicine was intuitive in its cruelties, that often it knew how much the body might stand in order to have another day of sun on the water, another taste of fresh peach. And so she was happy when he decided to move to a smaller place, could pack up his boxes and make himself wholly independent. Could answer the phone with a rising inflection—"Hi there"—glad of the day and the few short moments of connection.

ONE YEAR LATER, HE TOOK HER ON A TOUR OF HIS NEW terrain. Lunch at the Women's Civic League cafeteria, where the thrift shop was filled with homemade stuffed animals, quilted handbags, pot holders, and eyeglass cases. Down the hill toward the art museum, stopping along the way in the triangular park near the

Catholic church for a few words with a young priest. Then a quick look at the new exhibit. Back up the hill and past the law offices of his patent attorneys. Right turn by the grocery store. The last long four blocks home—four miles in all—to the small apartment in an inner-city project on Franklin Avenue.

Outside, the neighbors called hello—single mothers, retired nurses, the woman who kept a baseball bat on her balcony in case of intruders. Inside, he'd invented new furniture—cardboard boxes covered with Con-Tact paper to resemble wood. Stacked on top of each other, they made bookcases. Upside down, footstools. Old checkbook boxes were pigeonholes. His grandson's paintings on the wall.

He was happy with microwave dinners, as long as he could go out occasionally to the bistro he'd discovered in a not-yet-renovated area—the one where the waitresses had green or purple hair and Sunday brunch was an omelet with anything you could ever want. When his son George drove up from Washington, he'd take him out for dinner if he found a coupon in the newspaper. The German restaurant had a pressed tin ceiling and upscale food. The Brazilian was down-and-out, a bit seedy at the edges.

The black beans were authentic, but the rest was unfamiliar. The bartender was Italian.

Two years of borrowed time, and two new patents.

THERE IS A DISTANCE BETWEEN 1911 IN ALMA, MICHIGAN, and 1995 in Baltimore that spans more than the miles it took to get him there. He remembers his father forgetting to step on the brake of his first automobile, shouting "whoa." He remembers the farm with its few apple trees, remembers the icy thrill of horse-drawn sleighs and what it was like to canoe the wild reaches of the Upper Peninsula. He remembers the plums in his parents' backyard and the best way to fertilize melons. He remembers leaving home in his early twenties to test his wings at Yale, where he went to study physics but was fascinated by everything else: the lectures, the concerts, the plays, the speech by Norman Thomas. He remembers teaching high school mathematics and meeting the woman who would become his wife. He remembers how she typed his way through graduate school. He remembers her death. Before that, he remembers their life in upstate New York, the way his children hovered over each litter of newborn rabbits, the way he built his dry stone wall, then tore it down and moved it several feet, the way the men he worked

with always called him the "good doc." He remembers
all his inventions, the ones patented in the company's
name, and the endless cups of coffee needed to come
up with an idea. He remembers leaving that house on
Hamilton Street, with its long shadow of memory, to
find another life in Baltimore. He remembers coming
to that city determined to fight against its new baseball
stadium, and then the pleasure he had taking his son to
games in that same stadium. He remembers the
trips—to Germany and Scotland when he was a boy, to
England, to Brazil, to Austria and Samarkand and
Portugal. He remembers looking for Bertrand Russell's
house at the end of a narrow lane in Wales and his con-
versation with the old philosopher's gardener. He
remembers returning to Portugal just before
Christmas in 1994, meeting a woman from California
who was a Quaker, a liberal Democrat, a skeptic—too
perfect to be true. He remembers coming back from
that trip to his daughter's home, from which he was
taken to the hospital with anemia and congestive heart
failure. He remembers that her husband gave him a
radio for Christmas and that he listened to it, although
he had scorned the earphones they had told him
would help. He remembers never using the electronic
Scrabble dictionary they'd brought. He remembers

wanting to go home, back to his place in Baltimore, fussing until they let him go. And he remembers the doctors there who operated on his heart and sent him back to his lonely apartment. He remembers more anemia and more congestive heart failure and a new hospital and a new set of experts and another operation. Or rather, he remembers agreeing to another operation. They wheeled him in, he began to count backwards, and then he remembered nothing at all.

HIS DAUGHTER KNOWS THE REST OF THE STORY. SHE knows that he wouldn't let her call his doctor when she heard his faint voice at the other end of the wire, distorted with pain. She knows that he asked his neighbor not to tell her he'd been rushed in the ambulance that very same day. And she was angry at him. Angry because he was so stubborn, angry because, for the sake of his independence, he allowed her to be so worried. His operation and her son's wedding were scheduled at the same time, and she knows she did not know what to do. She knows that, when asked, he told her, "Do what I'd do." When she asked what that was, he said, "I'd go to the wedding." This from a man who did not come to either of her weddings and had always told her to elope.

So she went to the wedding. It was everything a wedding should be. And when it was over, his operation had been a success except that he'd had a stroke and would never wake up, and her brother was left there to tell them to stop the machines. According to his will, his body went to science.

She never saw his body. Never pinched him or shook him or screamed into his ears. Never kissed him and whispered and moaned. Never smoothed his combed and parted hair, never touched the lips or beseeched or entreated. Simply noted his death: June 13, 1995, sometime in the evening, alone. Simply noted his death for what he wanted it to be—one more step in the inevitable direction.

She steps back into memory. He's there, peripheral in every image, red beard at the edge of every photo, voice at the end of the line. He's there in the old gray Studebaker, turning into the drive. He's digging up the flowering quince. He's listening intently to the Army-McCarthy hearings on the radio in the kitchen. He's building his stone wall.

SOMETIMES SHE WISHES SHE'D FLOWN BACK TO BALTIMORE to be with him. She knows she will wish that for the rest of her life, though she cherishes her decision to honor life—his life—in her son's good marriage. She wishes she'd gone there and thrown open the door and taken him into her arms, this man who never held her, who rarely touched, who never said *love.* She wishes she'd forced the words out of his mouth—all his passions and regrets and even his dreams deferred—though she knows he would have been mute and distant. As always.

Suppose she had come back. Suppose she'd gone to the sterile room where the doctor was, just then, rolling away the machine. Suppose she'd watched as his body struggled through its one last physical exertion and went still, became only his body after all. Would she feel less guilt?

Here's what I think. If she had stood there in that moment, or the moments after, when he was both there and not there—the father she'd loved but without the mind that was so proud of her mind—she would not have moved. She would not have cried or kissed or whispered or touched or entreated. It would have felt familiar, that abandonment. They would have been familiar, those blue eyes that would not turn to me in pity. She would have looked past him, staring long and hard at his distanceless death.

BLACK

OVERNIGHT, THERE WAS EVIDENCE OF A BEAR IN THE raspberries behind the cabin—grass in turmoil and the bushes picked clean. But we never heard him. The British couple said they thought they saw a bear crossing the highway, looked like a large dog, they said, and the locals agreed. But we never saw it.

We hadn't seen a moose either (though the signs on every road read BRAKE FOR MOOSE and underneath "Hundreds of Collisions"), so we took the Moose Tour. This turned out to be a large vanload of people huddled together thirty-five miles south of the Canadian border, peering through windows in search of an animal we weren't even sure we'd recognize. *There, across the pond, is that a tree stump? Did it move?* Up and down Route 110A, through the swampy interior of northern New Hampshire, we looked for moose. Ninety-seven percent success rate, they told us. But what did they mean by success? On the map, there were place-names: Moose Brook, Indian River, Deer Mountain, Success Pond.

Then—up one last bumpy road on the outskirts of Dummer as sunlight retreated—there he was, standing motionless in the swamp, more moss than the moss itself, turning his huge head into the spotlight, mist-riddled and ethereal, caught in darkness so profound there was nothing left for him to do but fade back into the forest. Out of our element, what did we see but abstraction, black on black?

REQUIEM

Ask me whether
what I have done is my life.
—WILLIAM STAFFORD, "Ask Me"

EVERYTHING'S GONE. CHILDHOOD WASHED AWAY. THE
rabbits in their little hutch. The maple closest to the
house, cut down in its prime, a jungle of branches.
The flowering quince. Hopscotch chalked on the
sidewalk. Roller-skate keys. The voices of our play-
mates, ceded to time.

Gone, too, the village as we knew it. Lost to the
flood of 1972. Gone, now, the Presbyterian church on
Hamilton, the barber shop with the pressed tin ceil-
ing, Tillman's Drug Store, the 5 & 10. Everything torn
down in a frenzy to rebuild. Frenzy built of impa-
tience to get on with the business of living.

Nothing to see as it was before, except in the
mind's eye, where the inevitable distortion is one of
your own making. So you linger there, where the
men from the factory are lounging in the park at

noontime, waiting for the one o'clock whistle. Linger there where the sun filters through maples and the streets are cool and green. Wait for the acrid scent of burning leaves, distant but exact, coloring the autumn air. The fat wheels of your bicycle wheel on down past Olive Street, turn left at Imperial, brake in front of your friend Donna's house, and you walk through the door of your old, lost world.

Memory has a way of turning, of taking the child by the hand. Those summer evenings lengthened to a thin strand of wire, probing the long hours of dusk. Our father's freckled back as he prunes the forsythia or saws at the bottom branches of the blue spruce. His voice wafting out over the darkening neighborhood, calling us in to where the steamy rooms waited at the top of the stairs.

One day my father came home with a man named Otis. He'd picked him up hitchhiking and brought him home. He didn't even ask. Just told my mother to set another place at the table, and afterwards, that Otis would be staying overnight. George and I were shy in the strange man's presence. He seemed to know things—all about driving trucks and picking fruit. He was heading south, where the crops were just beginning to ripen. He figured he had a couple days of hitching to get there. He and my father had a conversation about peaches. They used words I'd never heard before, but my father acted as though he'd picked peaches himself in some other lifetime. I knew my grandfather had a farm—one they drove to from the village—but if they had peaches it was probably only one tree, with sporadic fruit at that. And my father had never picked for a living, more for fun and the added bonus of fresh food. Still, he had his garden. Beans and peas newly planted, strawberries swaddled in straw. Asparagus pushing through the ground, growing overnight into something mysterious and sexual. Another night or two and it would be too late, a blowzy tangle of frothy green. Gone to seed. His garden that claimed him, over and over, with its urgency.

In the morning, my father drove Otis to the bus station and bought him a ticket. I've sometimes wondered if Otis was really heading south. If his story was true, or just what he thought my father wanted to hear. All I know is my father sent him south and, who knows, maybe he reached the peaches. Or maybe he got off at the next stop and asked for a refund. It's possible he watched the land unfolding before him until he fell asleep, waking in a strange town, dusk falling, and decided to ride on into his new life.

Maybe my father knew that Otis might be lying, but wanted to show him what it was like to have someone believe his story. Wanted to give him the feel of truth. After he took him to the bus station, my father came home, changed his clothes, and went into the garden. Harvested a few more rocks, as he'd say, tossing them into a bushel basket. George and I climbed the apple tree—the closest thing we had to peaches.

Done. His life is done. But life is more than the doing. It's what we walk around with in our heads. It's what we've seen: sunset over the Tetons, pale mauve, color of wildflowers. It's what we've heard: oriole in the far maple by the fence, train at the crossing—going, gone. It's what we've tasted: ripe tomato, cold cucumber soup with dill, and—my father's favorite—steamed mussels, fresh from the sea. Or what we've felt: velvet brushed against the nap, mist like a fine rain rising from the waterfall. It's everything we've wanted to do but never could: a talk with Bertrand Russell, a trip on the Orient Express.

Odd little old man, walking the streets of Baltimore in his Chinese straw hat like an upside-down lampshade. Talking to the Rastafarian on the corner. Talking to the doorman. The director of the gallery. Odd little old man, calling up a history of causes.

Voted four straight times for Norman Thomas. Adlai Stevenson. Conscientious objector in World War II. Marched in Washington against the war in Vietnam. Card-carrying member of ACLU. NAACP. UNICEF. Habitat for Humanity. American Friends Service Committee. Southern Poverty Law Center.

That's what he did. Sometimes he taught us the names of flowers. Trees. Birds in flight. Sometimes he taught us small, practical lessons—like how to lash sticks or build a fire, how to find north when you're lost in the woods. Stories. In his stories, his family drives to North Dakota in a Model T. His great-uncle joins a German-speaking Union regiment in the Civil War. America comes alive. The dream of America. The lovely ongoing dream that fed his rectitude.

My father would not say what the river says. He would not say mountains, or stars. He would only say people—what people are capable of saying. He would only say logic and principle and speculation and desire. He would only say that I could do whatever I wanted to do. Could not see obstacle. Could not see compromise. Could not rest.

Let them rest. All the ones I've lost, and lose again in recollection. Give him peace. Absolve him of my vivid memory.

George and I climb the apple tree——the one my father held together with a chain when lightning split its forked trunk. Willed it into living. We edge our way out on the large limbs to where they begin to creak and sway. The bark underneath our fingers is old and smooth, worn smooth by our climbing, our slippery weight. We hide there in the camouflage, watching as he bends to pull the weeds near the new stalks of corn, stands up to wipe the sweat from his forehead, bends again. Watch as he balances the stones vertically along the top of his stone wall, fitting each in place as though it will be there a century later. Watch as he splits the cherry logs with his long-handled axe. Can almost smell their fragrance when, next winter, they will fill the rooms with this moment, when, small below us, he still seems larger than life. World. Without end.

IN THE END

In the end, the water was too cold for us.
——ROBERT LOWELL, "Water"

ON THE FERRY TO NORTH HAVEN, WE WATCH THE WATER
darken and go deep. We pass a naval ship, all hands on
deck, lining its sides in their white uniforms, their stiff
salutes. And then the island: a line of white houses
standing at alert above the bay, caught briefly
between the blue of the water, the same blue of the
sky. In his poem to Bishop, Lowell called them
bleak——bleak and "stuck" to the hill like oyster
shells. A sad poem, ending in resignation. This is the
place where he stood back, at the wrong end of the
telescope, watching the world unfold in miniature,
as though, once you were inside it, time had spaces of
its own. Perhaps it does.

"Remember?" Lowell asks. He is urgent. The poem
shouts its present tense. But he is already lost in the
past. "Remember?" The question mark implies a
moment shared; the verb inscribes its distance. It is

filled with *if only*—and who is to say whether Bishop included herself in his pronoun? In the end, revision was her mode, while his was recollection. Repeat, repeat, repeat: one moment held against the ocean's inescapable chill.

In Castine, sun glints on waves. Glitters. There is the white house. There, Blue Hill. Before today, they were only places in a poem, something to color its pages. But now, Blue Hill clearly in sight—a clear low rise of land covered with scrub brush, ordinary and wholly unredeemed—the seasons move. Bracken will rust and stain it red—the color of a fox arrested briefly in the headlights, the color of regret, if regret could be said to have one.

REMINDER

THERE HE WAS—THE IMAGE THAT STICKS IN THE MIND'S
eye—standing at the foot of a driveway on ROUTE 116
out of Jefferson, New Hampshire, August 4, 1997, 3:00
P.M. Of all the images of these mountains—clouds
rising from the valley, white farmhouses tucked
neatly into the hillsides, and everywhere, peripheral
and ever-present, the deep purple rim of mountain
against the sky—he is what I remember.

At first he was only a figure at the side of the road,
stepping from the forest, singular and surprising.
Holding a cardboard sign, probably a hitchhiker with
Boston or Albany or somewhere nearer at hand as his
destination. But when he heard the sound of our
motor, he swiveled, and the sign came clear. ON
STRIKE. At the foot of his driveway on a little-traveled
road, he was declaring his solidarity with the other
UPS drivers across the nation—his counterparts in
Somerville and Tucson and the hills of north Georgia.

This could be the hills of Georgia and the little roads
that veer off from Young Harris, on toward Brasstown

Bald. These could be those woods, though in August they would be smoldering with a hazy heat compared to this crisp New England air. But the mailbox set carefully at the end of the drive, the curve of dirt road up toward a small house, the young man in bluejeans and T-shirt, might be at home in either scene. What would differ is the food on the table, the manner of speech. Turn on the TV—they watch the same news; go into the mall—they buy the same shoes; flip on the radio—they'll hear the same songs. They are more alike today than they have ever been before.

Watch the ads—the package is being delivered in the Highlands of Scotland, a little seacoast town lost to history. The driver is looking for a Mr. Macleod. And of course there are seven Mr. Macleods, but the driver finds the right one and the job is complete. These could easily be the mountains of Scotland, though they lack their treeless subtleties. Still, winding our way through Crawford Notch, we could imagine ourselves on the way to Kyle of Lochalsh, rock rising steeply beside us and, in the distance, a purple haze of mountain after mountain. So maybe over there, somewhere outside Fort William, on a small one-laned road, a young man is standing with his sign of resistance.

Or outside Petropolis, where Brazilians go to imitate the Swiss, someone is painting the signs in Portuguese, and young men are fanning out into the mountains to keep their solitary vigils on more tropical roads ringed with the magenta blooms of impatiens, *Maria Sem Vergonia,* Mary Without Shame.

These places are one place in the mind that possesses them all. A palimpsest. Just as the coast of Maine, with its rocky shore and lobster boats, blurs into the inlet at Friday Harbor, and the San Juans, in turn, are like Skye. Water with hills in the distance, water and the wind-lashed land, the scoured blueberry hills that blend to stubborn moorland. The wind whines around your face and you push on into it, riddled with sensory memory locked in your body, visceral in its salty reminder. And then they differentiate themselves, sorted into particulars, into heather or hay field or blueberry flats. None of them home.

PORT TOWNSEND

AS FAR NORTH, MAYBE, AS WE CAN BE, HERE AT THE
uppermost tip of the country, but still not all the
way west, where the Pacific holds out other prom-
ises. Still, close enough to think ourselves alien to
the glaring headlines, the TV commentaries. Close
enough to feel that we might someday unfurl our
sails. Or, at the very least, board one of the pristine
ferries that gleam in the slant light and never get
off. Simply move between here and there, penin-
sula and island, over and over like a needle pushing
itself through cloth, stitching shore to shore. Green
trees, brown bluff, blue water, and, in the morning,
the gray of foghorns calling through mist. At night,
the clear cold colors of the stars. And the ferry's
lights, bright rhythm on the water, disbursing dis-
tance like a metronome.

MIX AND MATCH

It's a function of creative men to perceive the relations
between thoughts, or things, or forms of expression that
may seem utterly different, and to be able to combine
them into some new form.

—WILLIAM PLOMER

DAWN, ADIRONDACKS. MY FATHER'S PADDLE AT THE STERN
of the canoe. Sun creeping over the mountain. Sun
turning the river to molten glass, disturbed only by
the dip and pull, dip and pull. The little whirling vor-
tex where the paddle lifts, circular, distinct. The canoe
cuts the surface, slips through slate into silver into
gold as the sun bursts over the horizon and catches
each curve in its momentary glare. Morning birds.
Slish of paddle. My father is this quiet, this sure. The
land slides by his shoulder, fluid in its rush to recede.

WHAT OPENS THE HALF-DOOR OF REMEMBERED EXPER-
ience? Jogs it into motion? One moment I'm here,
locked in my life, and the next I'm walking with you

188 :: JUDITH KITCHEN

up the hill to Kate Kearney's Cottage. Matthew and Robin will be there, waiting. We'll listen to the music in the next room, where the fiddler says he doesn't know "The Kerry Dancers." My mother's voice will call to me—*oh to think of it, oh to dream of it*—filling my own heart with the press of memory. Can they hear her, those who never heard her, hardly able to carry a tune, but filled with this tune from so far away? Do they know why I request the song, why I'm disappointed? What will they ask for to carry them back to this evening, the long walk home, our flashlights shining on the lane and, ahead of us, the yellow door of the cottage we now call "home," though we know we will leave here tomorrow?

MY UNCLE MILES, WHO IS REALLY A SECOND COUSIN, takes my brother George and me for a tractor ride around the farm in Michigan. He stops to let us watch the pigs rooting in the far field. So I balance with my feet on the lowest rail, my hands trailing over the top of the fence to reach toward one large sow. She makes snorting noises—*snrrllg, snrrllg*—lacking vowels, and slightly menacing. The sky arches overhead, larger than sky is supposed to be, and in the background the tractor tugs with its growl, let's go, let's get going. But my hand lingers on the wooden rail, feels the splinters, the rough surfaces of my mother's childhood. My Uncle Miles had a twin brother, Marion, my mother's other cousin, but he killed himself long ago. I look at the back of my uncle's head, wondering whether he misses someone who looked like himself, someone who knew him going and coming, someone who shared memory like the other half of the sandwich. I look at the back of his head, then up into an enigmatic sky.

CORR BAILE (IRISH). THE BEND FOR HOME. SOMETHING SO old it's been given a name. Ever will be. A house, just around the corner, and inside, people and stories to balance the equation. Voices. Or silence. Comfort of the familiar. My dog Tray sleeping in her place behind the sofa. The thump of her tail. The click of the furnace. The heat from the hot air register. Verbless. Held in the mind without chronology. Dermot Healy calls it the "time that can't be given back, but is, continuously." The road bends, and you round the curve.

UNDER THE TREE, THERE'S A DRY SPOT WHERE THE RAIN doesn't reach. A circle of dryness, as if it were falling through the willing rain. If you stand there, you can hear the steady plink on the leaves overhead singing alto to your thoughts. Outside the circle, the ground is rinsed in steady sound. After a while, you begin to think in time with the growing insistence of the rain. When you feel the first drop break through, a touch on your cheek, you shiver.

MY MOTHER'S HANDS ON THE PHONOGRAPH RECORD. the brush in her hands. The sound of the bristles in the grooves. The angry sound of her scrubbing, scrubbing. Washing the silt from her music. Silt from the flood that filled the first story of her home on Hamilton Street. The home she moved to because it couldn't have a flood, not like the one on River Road. The home she made—canning peaches in the deep water bath till they emerged golden in sunlight, weeding the rock garden to make room for primrose and violet, ironing the Thanksgiving tablecloth until it settled on the cherry table like a field of snow. But simile is the present—the observer making connections, one thing to another, one way of seeing in the here and now. When will the sound of her scrubbing subside?

TAKE THE POEMS OF A SOLDIER——WILFRED OWEN——AND the music of a pacifist—Benjamin Britten—and combine them with the Catholic Mass for the dead. Add the distanced voices of the boys' chorus, remote as time itself. Open the skies above Coventry Cathedral to the sound of trumpets. Let the bombs abate in memory. Let us sleep now. This is metaphor. Is music set to words. Is ritual that takes us back to what we've always known. Into the interior, the bone, the bread of sorrow.

"THIS IS THE SEA THEN, THIS GREAT ABEYANCE," SAYS Plath in "Berck-Plage," setting the tone of the poem. A friend is dying. A friend is dead. The sea goes on, relentless, relentless. The landscape of the moment—sea, sanatorium, rainy churchyard—is the language of the soul. An old man is vanishing, like the troughs between waves, like the hollows between hills, like the flicker of the curtain in the window, the pallor of the flowers that fly off "into nothing." The coffin is blessing, holds a "marvelous calm." Stilled to perception, the poet mourns in the only words she can find for mourning, her own face wordless and slow in the pouring rain as she reaches past simile, past the moment of observation, into the self, the shaped wood of metaphor. This is grief, singular and significant, given its proper place in the place-names of the world.

DAWN. ADIRONDACKS. MY FATHER'S PADDLE AT THE stern of the canoe. He sets it deep and pulls long, twisting the paddle outward at the end of his stroke, then lifts it up and feathers it through the air. His stroke is so powerful it matches two of mine in the bow, and even then I can't keep the canoe from veering. That's why he twists the paddle, to help hold it steady. We head into the sun, into the breaking day. The river shimmers in light that spreads over it like cloth unfolding. The day is ahead of us, filling the spaces on the map with the solitary *knock-knock* of a woodpecker, the *maybe* of a deer come down to drink, thick deciduous forest that seems, the deeper we go, to open itself to our secrets.

IT ALL MOVES BACK TOWARD METAPHOR. HUNGERS FOR what is known before there are words to break it into sense. Moves toward the primary color of experience. Mix and mix, the colors mute and conform. The oboe blends with clarinet. But the mind refuses the easy bridge of simile, refuses a world made whole with universal truth. Truth is a lie, is all the lies we've ever told. We dive back down to find the place where the infinite adjectiveless world explains itself.

GEORGE IS OUTSIDE THE WINDOW, FRAMED IN SNOW. HIS bright blue hat stark against the white that makes everything sharper. Soon he will throw himself down in it, flap his wings. Soon he will scoop it up and pack it tight, almost to ice, and throw the snowball at the window. It will hit with a thunk, break apart, slide slowly down past the sill, except for the sticky center that clings, even now, to the glass.

LOOK HARD. BONNARD CALLED THE PAINTING *THE BOWL of Milk,* but the eye scans left to right, top to bottom, before it finds the bowl, almost hidden in the folds of the girl's skirt, color of skirt, in the moment before she sets it down, outside the frame, for the black cat at her feet, nearly invisible. The title calls our attention to what is variable, what is fluid and fleeting. Its color is an echo of the flowers in the vase, also in shadow, whose petals will drop one by one to the cloth. The eye is not interested in the bowl, the flowers fading. The eye is drawn to sunlight on the tabletop, stilled to constancy, so solid it becomes the afternoon you'd almost forgotten.

WHEN YOU SIT ON THE HANDLEBARS OF MY UNCLE RAY'S bicycle, the wind catches in your hair. He makes the wind. You seem to stand still, held in the crook of the handlebar, your legs in the basket, your arms holding tight. Light scores your eyes. You want to retain the moment forever, caught between daylight and dusk, cut like a silhouette, everything heightened, heady with loss.

TODAY, ON THE CAR RADIO, A FOLK SONG SUNG SO sweetly you could feel the words crossing the sea, the mouth forming the shaped sound of the word and the music lending it substance. At the end of the song, the announcer said it was sung by Benjamin Britten. Who knew he had this clear tenor tone, these rounded syllables to drive him back through abstract notes, the f♯ of felt words finding their place in the scale of things? Who knew he could sing his way back through time to where his love was waiting?

"IF I EVER HAVE A MISTRESS, IT WILL BE THE CANYON," says Barry Goldwater, turning from the camera to look out over miles and miles of rippling rock. The camera returns, then, to his own photographs. Portraits of light. *Navajo Women,* taken in the 1930s—three women blending into the canvas of stony ground that holds them there, shadow spilled across their wrinkled faces until they harden into tacit history.

MY SON WILLIAM SETS THE WORDS OF HOPKINS'S "Inversnaid" to music, mixes the song on his multi-track recorder, matches the longing he hears to his own love for the land: "What would the world be, once bereft / Of wet and of wildness? Let them be left, / O let them be left, wildness and wet; / Long live the weeds and the wilderness yet." Simple words that connect us to the passionate priest, white house rising across Loch Lomond like an invitation to the poem. But we forego the ferry, hurry on down to Glasgow, fail to go in search of "headbonny ash" or "windpuff-bonnet of fawn-froth." Because we feel in the "despair to drowning" the geography of the words that sing to us over the century. O let them be left—wildness and wet: words on their way to becoming.

ALERT BAY

SEEN FROM THE BOAT, THE TOTEM POLES SEEM TO RISE
out of the water like a forest of faces. What they are
is the cemetery at Alert Bay, a place sacred to the
Kwakiutl and not available to tourists. And this is a
landscape begging for totems, for story and legend to
match the trees that dominate the hillsides, reaching
right down to the shoreline. These totems are
faded—faded and weathered as the Danes who set-
tled this region and could not survive its winters.

After the desolation of the last one hundred
miles—not one car in either direction, only a log-
ging truck, immense on the winding road—the boat
seems civilized. It slices the sea like a knife. Entering
the space near Robson Bight, our guide cuts the
engines, and we begin our search for whales. Orcas
travel in pods and this is a resident pod, so he's famil-
iar with them all. When, on the starboard side, one
pushes his head out of the water, seems to hold his
pose as if for a hidden camera in a gesture known as
"skyhopping," our guide is able to tell us that this is

G-9, the largest of the males. How does he know? The other males have been given similar numbers——G-3, G-7——but the females are called Bess and Lucy. They swim around the boat, playful and inquisitive. They flirt with us, hardly what we'd call killer whales.

The transient pods, however, are known to attack the resident pods. They recognize each other through their differing dialects. The calls of the residents of northern British Columbian waters are very different from those of residents of southern British Columbian seas. In sharp contrast, the same dialect is shared by transient whales from Alaska to Monterey Bay.

Later, when we pass the totems on our return to Telegraph Cove, we see them in new light. Unlike in the museum, where they've been tamed to anecdote, to words on the placard that fix them in wooden detail, the bared teeth and suggestion of fin are now essence of water, essence of wind.

RICHLAND

no rain scarcely ever falls in these plains
and the grass is short and but thin.
—MERIWETHER LEWIS

THE RAIN SHADOW AT THE EASTERN EDGE OF THE
Olympics has given way to the lush rain-fed coun-
tryside along the Columbia. Clark described a great
rapids, now covered by water backed up by the
Bonneville Dam. We're driving east at last, heading
for home, keeping water in sight for as long as we
can. Still, there's a place where water gives out and
the arid desert of eastern Washington begins. Circles
of green where the rolling irrigation pipes have plot-
ted their slow compass. And otherwise, the dried
browns and tans of things about to blow away.

Rising out of the flat land, the water towers and
grain elevators of Richland. Nothing on the map for
miles in any direction. Only two large highways
intersecting here, at the height of folly. Scrawled in
neon, motels at every junction. Papery, windswept

motels with flimsy walls and faded railings. Three
children and a soccer ball. A pool flecked with leaves
that must have come from somewhere. Trucks by
the hundreds.

In town, we discover Texas John's—truck stop to
end all truck stops, flanks of trucks and a phone at
every table. There's barbecued ribs and corn bread
and beans and almost anything that might remind
you of Texas, especially if you'd never been to Texas.
Home away from home. Music from the fifties and—
lo and behold—a jukebox for every table. There's
even the flip side of "Heartbreak Hotel," which has
always been my favorite.

I'm rolling now, back through my life to when I
twirled my crinolines to that one tune. I was the one
who taught her to love, and I learned how to love,
my hand on his cheek, his hand at my back, steering
me through time as though history itself was
parched and only that singular, dusk-filled voice
could summon the rain of remembrance.

STANDARD TIME

WE'VE STOPPED SAVING DAYLIGHT. NOW, IN THE DARK
diminished hour of five o'clock, light hovers some-
where over the lake, a second horizon floating
above the first, bright for a lingering moment, then
gone. It comes again in early morning—earlier
morning—when we don't yet want to be awake.
Oh we know that it helped our grandparents on
the farm, helped them milk and feed in the milk-
light of a November sunrise, but we have left all
that behind.

Daylight. Day delight. The calypso of four years
old, early to rise into the dawn. The wide expanse of
lawn where the conscientious objectors planted
their long rows of lettuce. More than a victory gar-
den: feeding the war, but not fighting it. Scud and
scuffle of hoes, my father showing them how to lift,
then pull against the grain. My brother in his three-
wheeled baby buggy. No rubber for a fourth wheel.
And down the road, Johnny Haar, gassed in World
War I, his face twisted into a smile. Drool down his

chin, and his indecipherable sounds. Not quite a wail, not quite a moan, though my mother says *see how happy he is.*

Not a farm, but next door to a farm. Cornfields and pasture. Cows restless in their stanchions. *Mooooo.* They really do sound like the storybooks. Shifting of rumps. The call rises at the far end of the barn. Clank of metal as the cow swings her head, backfeet splayed. A ripple of flanks. *Moooo.* The answer, close now, louder, slobber of sound.

That was all before. When everything rose early. A rooster who haunted the rafters. When everything seemed large and familiar and unchanging. Then there was kindergarten and the world grew as small as a word. C-o-w. Which led to h-o-w and v-o-w. Which led in turn to the confusion of *low* and *mow* and *sow* and *tow.* And back to *now.* And later *bough* and *through* and *tough* and *thorough.* Small as a word, and unfamiliar.

⌒

Dawn over the Cascades. Three thousand miles away, I see it happen. Though I know you really can't see the mountains till noon. Gray in the morning, a filtered gray, all gauze and cautious cloudcover. Three thousand miles and three time zones, and still I can call up sunlight on snowcap.

Sundown, nightfall: the compound words of active disappearance. I picture the Olympics, their dark serrated edges outlined in pink and gold. And then the solid dark. Eleven o'clock, which only days ago was midnight: the motion-sensored light in the backyard snaps on. My brother opens the sliding glass door and looks out. Raccoons, he thinks. So he listens for something—a rattle of lids, a scratch of claws on the cement patio. I see myself in the premature light of morning, looking for evidence. What was out there in the night? My imagination includes the raccoon, the deer that stare back unafraid, apples falling behind the fence, the last long stretch to the solstice. This, I suspect, is nostalgia for the future.

Two hundred years ago, a day had its own slow cycle, full and round as the arc of the sun in the sky. No one conceived of today's digital dislocation. And then, with the Industrial Revolution, suddenly time belonged to someone else. The world shifted. Protestant time: doctrinal and unrepentant.

The long reach back to four years old—conjured memory—is not the same as nostalgia, which presumes a sense of time passing, the sense of self that says *mine, my time, my time,* over and over, a litany of hours. No, that was before time slipped through the fingers and made itself felt in its very dissipation. The sun rose, and fell. The men came with their tools, went back again to their quarters. My mother took down the clothes from the line with their hint of folded sunshine. My father came home from work and took up his hoe. Up one row, down another. What is a weed? What is a sun-ridden sky, and a world beyond it?

Time stops. Suspended there where to sit all afternoon on the front step is simply to sit all afternoon on the front step. Is to register the sound of duration in birdcall and breeze. Is to hear the blurred wings of a lawn mower, a dog punctuating the silence from two blocks away. One bark. A syncopated beat. Then two more. Then nothing. But a nothing full of the bark that did not follow, an ellipsis of sorts. And then, when you least expect it, when the throb of sunshine is all you can sense, another bark. Fainter, and less insistent.

Afternoons filled with time, as though it were solid and you could save it in your pocket. As though you could part it, like a curtain, and find yourself inside another room. Sometimes you did. You stepped right inside the pages and they held you up. Wherever you were, the book was all that contained you as you clambered over the locked garden wall. It knew you better than you knew yourself.

⤳

But some books were better than others. You knew enough to know that, even then. Some took the words that had floated free above you and anchored them to circumstance. The wall grew thick with vines. It became your secret.

Some were better than others, and you held the key—a huge black key that turned in the lock and allowed you entry. Indeterminate time, until your mother called you back for dinner, until bedtime came in its lockstep pace.

Those were the books that mattered. They were in you, the way waves, incessant, after a while cease to be heard. Even now, you can call up their timelessness. Not only *The Secret Garden* and *Little House on the Prairie,* but the chronicle of your maturation: *East of Eden, The Great Gatsby, Light in August*—west and east and south opening themselves to you long before you mounted the steps of the train, long before the summer you and your friend drove her sister's old Renault into Wyoming, where you had to wait two days for foreign tires to be shipped to Dubois from Cheyenne. West and east and south, and suddenly there you were: in

Dublin itself, its wet streets slick and shiny in the streetlights, seeming to leap from the pages of Joyce. Were you really there, or did the book take visible shape? You shivered a little in the rain and were glad of its physical reminder. You stepped back into time, into deadline and decision and detail.

⌒

Who were those men from the C.O. camp? They came from Brooklyn, from Buffalo and Pittsburgh, brought together in our town through their shared refusal. Some were communists—innocent idealists of the sort that only America can produce. They were city men who knew nothing of farming. If they'd been from the West, we know they would have been pressed into fighting fires, building dams, clearing trails in the national parks. But in the East, they were herded into a barracks and farmed out to do their farming. My father was one of them.

Or not one of them, not quite. He was a physicist in a necessary job, so he was allowed to stay at home, allowed to go to work each day. He moved freely in and out of society. The best of both his worlds. By rights, they should have resented him.

I would have sensed it. I'd have felt their backs stiffen when they tossed me into the air. I'd have seen their eyes cloud over whenever he came home, riding his bicycle the long seven miles, saving gasoline. They would have looked away, busy with their weeding. Instead, they looked up, called out the latest news on the radio. And they welcomed his hoe, adding to the rhythm of the long summer evening. Light languished. None of them knew—not even my father, the physicist—that Los Alamos was looming.

Here's what they thought: all wars are the same, and all are inhuman.

Some books are better than others. I say it into the void. I say it into an atmosphere filled with the explosive shards of theory. I say it in the face of a vocabulary that daunts even the dauntless, a jargon I cannot wrest from its abstract origins. Some books are better than others. They know more of the human heart, and more of its heartlessness. They are haunted by water. Haunted by what they cannot escape. Heart-rending. They are not cultural constructions. They are Johnny Haar—the pure, individual cry of the singular first person. His war was not the same—and it was inhuman. Time twists and conjoins like a Möbius strip, catches up from behind and places its shoes in its own parenthetical footprints.

We could name them: those brave voices that stand out from the crowd. We could name them, but our lists would not tally. Still, we would know what we mean: someone was there before me. Some one.

⁂

The body wakes in its old time zone. Shaken awake. All afternoon you sat on the step while the sun swept the sky. All afternoon you relived time. Dean Stockwell played Colin, you remember that. And now you see him on the screen, an aging man, a few years older than you are. Your mirror, if you needed one. Though anything will do: "Blue Suede Shoes" or "Wayward Wind"; paper dolls, the Brooklyn Dodgers, s&h Green Stamps. Green War Savings Stamps. My father's yard laid out in tidy rows: corn and carrots and onions and beets. The handwriting of a generation.

Yesterday the tall young woman who didn't know how to hold a pen. Caught it up in her fist, then twisted her wrist in order to print a couple of words. Where was the Palmer Method of her youth? That spiral of Os uncoiling like a slinky. Something lost, something skittering away. So this is what it is to see time fly. To count the years, then the months, then the days. To feel the press of time even as the minutes quicken, even as everything moves in doublespeed, fastforward, a race to the finish.

Now there is only the page—and the way the day stops at the brink of it. You have no words for what the greatest writers do, and hardly any words for how they do it. But you know what it is to turn back the hands of the clock, stare out of your bedroom window into one long evening hour when the men are leaning on their hoes, talking softly about everything that will matter for the rest of your life. The heft of their words, the urgency of tone as they talk about missing their wives, about violence and war and the way they have had to look deep into their own capacities. And then your mother calls through the screen—coffee and cake—and they all come, laughing, into the house. Their sounds will weave through fifty years, faded and forgiving. You've forgotten their names: those men who would not fight. You wonder if they might have been mistaken. You know that you don't know what drove their moments of decision. All you can hear is the grate of metal on rock, the small *harumph* as a clump of dirt is pulled from the aggregate. The war ended, and they went away. The mouse ran down. You went off to school.

PROPORTION

SING *LOO*, MISS WITZEL COMMANDED, SHAPING THE
sound into one round flute. I could hear the sound ris-
ing above me, perfect in its ability to match her tones. I
could hear where my voice was supposed to follow. *Loo,*
I answered, my voice flat and unchanged, so clearly only
my voice. I was hopeless. She made it clear that I was
hopeless. "You can simply mouth the words," she said.

But the sounds were so clear in my head, the way,
even now, I can reproduce Elvis mumbling
"Heartbreak Hotel" right down to its least articulated
"muhmuhmuh baby." The way I can hear the high
notes of the boys' choir in York Cathedral, their
soprano tinged with what their voices would
become, a shadowy understory of reserved depth.
The way the tenor in Benjamin Britten's *War Requiem*
sings "Let us sleep now," pulling the long *e*s of sleep
into another half-syllable, a lullaby sung by a dead
man to his slayer, a catch in the throat of time.

So it's not that music eludes me, but that I elude it.
I fail it, time and time again, even on those rare times

when I lose my inhibitions and belt out a song with the car radio. Why doesn't my voice follow the sure lead of the singer, up and down in measured leaps, the ones I hear in my head but cannot reproduce with my vocal cords?

My body never fails me in little things—the confidence with which I aim my croquet ball and—chunk—clip my opponent's ball, shove it just out of play. Or the way I can sort silverware, without error, fork, knife, fork, fork, spoon, into the drawer. Or the way I can balance on a railroad track, quick little steps down its tightrope before I hop again to the ties with their awkward spaces, their short, short, long, short, long, to keep you going. And when I was young I could turn cartwheels and flips, stretch myself into a split. Even now, I can bend over and touch my hands to the floor—not just the fingertips, but the whole hand—and my knees never bend. So why, when the music's turned on, when everyone dances and sways and begins to shuffle their feet, do I know that I won't be swaying in the same direction? won't be able to twirl when his hand sets me spinning?

HERE'S THE SCENE: OCTOBER 19, 1995. I'M IN OKLAHOMA, at Quartz Mountain, where I've been working on writing with people who survived the bombing of the Murrah Building. There's a hot wind blowing, scouring the land, rubbing it raw without cleansing. I'm tired. I'm emotionally exhausted. For sheer pleasure, I'm singing with the gospel chorus because that's one time I can't do anything but be. Can't listen to another story. Can't try to put myself where I can't imagine—husband with missing hands, daughter disappeared in seven stories of rubble. I'm singing my heart out, songs I don't believe, words I don't for one minute believe or even want to believe. Jesus is my Savior. God will heal my pain. And I don't hold back because nobody knows the trouble I've heard all day long and here I have forty minutes of pure music to take it back and make it right. Except for one thing—the clapping.

It turns out that I can't clap and sing at the same time. Everyone else is clapping when my hands are silent. Then my clap—loudly solitary—comes at the offbeat. Or the onbeat, I'm not sure which. Anyway, I try to adjust. But soon there it is again, my lonely clap when everyone else is swaying. It also turns out that I can't clap and *pretend* to sing because there's the same problem. The only solution is to sing and pretend to clap. But even then I could be seen to be out of time. So it's best if I "simply fake the claps" and stand behind someone so no one will notice. That way I can pretend to sing, too, when it's necessary. But if I stand next to Lula, it's okay, because her voice will take mine wherever she wants to take it. She's that sure, that filled with whatever spirit is needed to keep me going.

WHEN MY SON MATTHEW BEGAN VIOLIN LESSONS, I WAS informed that I would have to help him keep in tune. My heart sank. Poor kid. But in the end, it wasn't hard. The inner ear, where melody moves so perfectly, worked fine. "A bit sharp," I'd tell him, and his finger would move imperceptibly down the string until it was perfect. I could hear it. And so could he— heard it until his fingers knew exactly where to go, how to make the bow hesitate slightly until the music was caught on an upsweep, expectant and alive. Even today, I see him listen intently to the way the fiddler catches eight hundred years of Irish grief, then reproduce it in a rush of American enthusiasm. I can't do that—can't cross the bridge from head to finger.

When I took music lessons—both piano and flute—I was an arithmetician, not a mathematician. Each note held the exact time indicated on the page, a wooden reproduction of what someone else must have heard as living. The notes went up and down, my fingers deftly striking the key or covering the hole I'd memorized, no problem there. But they didn't sing. They simply counted out the time like a melodic metronome.

I've heard the recorder played as I would long to play it—pleading, plaintive, or capering through a meadow of song. And the pennywhistle, with its flourishes, the fingers flicking the quiver of air. The song rises finished, completed by something human and understandable, something I cannot find inside myself, though I swear I know it when I hear it.

JUST AS I KNOW GOOD ART WHEN I SEE IT. KNOW SOMEthing that happens outside the frame, outside the time (which is the now) of the picture. Know that the painting isn't about the landscape or the shapes or even the light, though they are all a part of it, but about the longing the painter feels when he sees that blue door, the one he can't enter, but knows, with a certainty that translates itself through the brush, that if he could enter, there would be warmth and a bowl of fruit on the table and he might never need to leave again.

Because that's in the painting, in the brush strokes that evoke the light, that shade the patches of snow into blue echoes of the door and then take the eye upward to where the sky which might offer solace is also white and wide with desire. The whole world wants to enter that one patch of color, that stab of paint that sucks at light with its own insistent longing.

But how does the artist know that a square of color, a streak of white, will resolve itself when the viewer stands back? How does he learn to move the outside world inside, then give it back in intricate dabs of paint? He lets us into his way of seeing, his way of reconstructing what we can only observe, watch as it fades and disappears. There they are—caught in the moment of their being—irises so ripe they carry with them the reek of decay, or peonies in their brief, blowzy decadence, spilling over the lip of the blue vase—caught in the moment just before their petals will spill on the lavender tablecloth like last night's spilled wine. So the painting carries the future inside its ever-present present, carries what we know of the world and what the artist senses of impermanence. It carries his desire to hold it all, to fill with the overbounty of earth remembered.

Even abstract paintings—the ones I like—carry with them memory of what it is to be alive. Rectangular fields of green under strips of sky. I think to myself, I've been there. Even fields of red under a yellow sky, I've been there too.

Or the bitter realism of Hopper, where, even if I haven't been there, I've imagined the lives he's imagined. I've longed for that room filled with that bright, exhaustible light.

MY SON WILLIAM BUYS PAINT, LARGE TUBES OF PRIMARY colors that he will mix on his palette. He goes to the arboretum each day at seven P.M. to catch the azaleas at dusk, just after their glory in the sun, just before they fade into the background noise of evening. Or else he spends the day with his notebook, brief moments sketched in pencil, waiting for his imagination on the canvas, his inventive flow of caricature and color which turns the known world into cartoon of radiator, radio, clock.

I remember when he was little, how he would throw himself on the sidewalk to watch the "red bug," the one we couldn't see, didn't believe, until we knelt on his level and—there it was—miniscule on the big world of the pavement. Or when he wouldn't build a tower for the pediatrician who wanted to measure his intelligence until the doctor gave him three *green* blocks, as though they had finally agreed, somehow, on the aesthetic importance of color.

My own ability to draw is limited to two essential doodles, both flowers, neither anything like a real flower. One has a round center and four petals, a short winding stem, two fat lilypad leaves at the bottom. The petals can be shaded in while talking on the telephone. The other is a direct copy of a flower painted in watercolor by a young Navaho painter called Beatien Yazz, a tall stem with leaves like fronds, a flower that spills from its tip like a waterfall in three curving petals. Whatever southwestern plant it represents is unknown to me.

Once I found one of my childhood drawings in the attic, saved by my mother, I guess. It was, of course, of a horse—dream horse in a field, beside a fence. His name was Prince. He was meticulously drawn, ears thrown forward in concentration, mane neat and combed, hooves carefully placed on the sloping terrain. But his midsection (if horses can be said to have midsections) was so out of proportion that it looked as though he would need another set of legs to hold it up—he was so much longer than he was tall. In fact, he reminded me of something I once saw in Goodland, Kansas—THE WORLD'S LARGEST SPERM WHALE. In sweltering heat, in the middle of a parking lot in the most landlocked part of the country, you paid a dollar and entered a refrigerated tractor-trailer, where, behind glass covered with blue cellophane to represent the ocean, you walked past a whale's head, the length of the truck past a "body" of burlap, and then came out by the tail. The body, the sign said, had had to be removed, but the burlap was supposed to be the exact length of the whale. Length, maybe, but it lacked substance. Something substantial, like the smear of oil that resolves itself in William's paintings, saying I was here, this is what the world has been to me.

MANY YEARS AGO, I TRIED POTTERY. IT WAS THE CLOSEST thing I could think of to Barbara Hepworth's smooth shapes in wood. Wood seemed impenetrable, but clay seemed possible. At least for a while. I remember my teacher's name was Lowell. That sounded like the right kind of name for a teacher of sculpture, which is how I was secretly thinking of pottery.

I learned to work the clay, pounding and kneading until the air was eased out of it. And I learned to shape it into a ball, something orderly and clean. I learned to swing my leg rhythmically to keep the wheel spinning, and to wait for the right speed to place my watery hands on the clay and begin to push down, to center it on the wheel, and then the exact time to begin, slowly, with thumb and forefinger to press the clay down and out, forming the rim of the vessel, to pull it carefully up, all the while spinning and spinning, shaping it, molding it to the shape in my head. Or almost. Mostly, the clay did what it wanted and I followed along, trying helplessly to keep it from collapsing and falling into the center in a hopeless mess. So my beautiful jugs had spouts where one was never intended, or what was once, in the mind, a tall and elegant vase became an ashtray after the fact. Well, so shape wasn't my métier. I'd try for color.

Chemistry, that's what glazing is all about. And I'd been good at chemistry. I enjoyed the mixing of the glazes, the colors I knew could be produced—*were* produced so perfectly in the mind. I saw the jug transformed with one slash of cobalt blue, an echo of the shape of the spout, there, on the other side. And the ashtray would be elegant in its own right, creamy, with a streak of rust. I painted the glazes stiffly onto the clay in the shapes I imagined.

When they came out of the kiln, I could never recognize my own pots. They were shrunken and dull. There was none of the flare I imagined. Nothing spontaneous.

AFTER TWO YEARS OF LESSONS, I DECIDED I WAS SUFFIciently advanced to let my husband try his hand. It was something we could do together, I thought, and I'd know more than he did. But it only took two lessons for Lowell to transfer his loyalty and his interest. *His* pots rose easily under his hands, took lovely shapes and seemed to do his bidding. *His* glazes—he was sloppy and slapdash—came out with the carefree air of something finding its proper form. I didn't give up, at least not then, though I gave some thought to needlepoint, which was Lowell's second love. I bought a pillow he'd designed, but it was clear there was too much work in it for even Barbara Hepworth.

I dreamed of Henry Moore. He knew a shape when he saw it. I'd seen an exhibit of all the small stones and sticks and shells he'd picked up and kept in his studio. They looked like miniature Henry Moore's. But how did he know what part of nature held his shaping hand? Whenever I've picked up a stone, it's usually been in a stream, catching my eye with its glint of color, its perfect shape. At home in a drawer, it looks like all the others, dusty and dulled to extinction. I can't remember where I found it, why I brought it home. Can't find its distinctive color, even a hint of interest.

What would wood do under my hands? Would it find its silken linings, its contours and planes, its solid sense of belonging? I hadn't the heart to begin.

PHOTOGRAPHY SHOULD BE FOOLPROOF, OR SO I THOUGHT when I decided to take it seriously. I was living in Brazil, a young mother terrified and bored at the same time. I was lost in my loss of language. My stomach was hollow for huge parts of each day. Where was I, who was I, what was I doing?

So I borrowed a camera and asked a friend—not really a friend, but someone I'd met who spoke English and had lived there three years and seemed at least more content than I felt and had a leather couch and didn't miss Thanksgiving—to teach me what she knew. She had a darkroom in her apartment, so she must have been serious. She began with light meters and f-stops. This appealed to my scientific nature—measurements were something I could handle. Then she suggested I just shoot and we'd develop the film and I'd learn from what I had done. So, briefly, Brazil became less frightening. I took photographs of light filtering through palm trees, splayed out like fingers. I captured the derelict men who slept each night on the sidewalk outside the shop at the corner, their sleepy-eyed waking when the shopkeeper shook them awake, and away. I shot the swings in a moment of rest, the scuffed ground beneath them, the shadows lengthening to indicate the end of afternoon. I caught the flags trailing from car windows when the soccer team won, the trail of cars sweeping the praça, all movement that seemed to suggest the honking of horns. I thought black and white, shadow and light, filigreed wrought-iron table on shiny tiled patio, dark church door across the square, crooked masts rising above moored boats.

When I got to the darkroom, we took out the film. I'd put it in wrong; it had never wound through the camera. All the photos I'd seen were lost to me then, though they shape themselves now in perfect memory.

Since then I've bought cameras as presents for others. *They* can take the pictures. I'll try to remember the moment as it is, not as someone wants it to be.

Hold still. Smile. Move a little to the left. But I want the day intact. Moving in the mind with the exactitude of fact. Moving through the mind like water, coloring the stones of memory. *They* hide behind cameras, trap time on film to be handled and fondled and held at bay. I want to wade in, to stand where the light fans through the branches. To hear the one last bird call before you know it's the last, before you realize that silence has settled in for the night.

SO WHAT HAVE I OMITTED? DANCE. THOUGH DANCE IS related to music, so you can imagine my problems. When I was little, I took ballet lessons, though they were mostly gymnastics and Russian folkdance, until you graduated to toe shoes, and then I wasn't very interested any more. In high school I jitterbugged my way through the sock hops and I can still make my feet work a syncopated beat, though I prefer the slow dance where two bodies seem to learn from each other where they have to go. "Blue Moon." "Great Pretender."

The body gets in the way. You imagine yourself lithe, hardly in need of practice, ready to respond. You imagine yourself expressive, your body the face of the song. You imagine yourself light, lighter than I'll ever be.

Let me tell you a story about dance. Three summers in a row I was supposed to dance with Garth Fagan, who was then well on his way toward becoming Garth Fagan Dance, rave choreographer of New York City, winner of a Tony for *The Lion King*. We were working at a teachers' institute in Rochester, New York, giving them immersion in the arts. Garth came to my writing classes—and he wrote. I was supposed to come to the dance classes—and dance. And every day there was some reason, some excuse. I didn't bring leotards. I needed to find a Xerox machine. I was working on my lesson. I was late. I was early. I wasn't available.

I hid from Garth Fagan. I did not want to give my overweight body over to him. I did not want the teachers to see me failing where I wanted so badly to succeed. I did not want to feel myself clumsy and awkward and out of tune.

One year there was a teacher who must have weighed twice what I did. At least. But she had no choice. She had to dance. My first thought—what was Garth going to do with her? Only after that did I think to think how brave she was, how I admired her. But I was embarrassed for her too. What would she do on the day they all demonstrated their choreography?

I was hiding, so I didn't see what Garth was doing. Didn't know he had chosen her group for his own. Didn't see him practicing, working his seven teachers through to a finished shape. The day of the perform-ance, there she was. Not a part of the chorus, not hidden in the background, but featured with a solo. The others danced to her lead, made sense of her slow and gracious movements. She was beautiful. Radiant. Everything in proportion.

HERE'S THE SCENE: I'M IN OKLAHOMA. I'M SINGING with the gospel chorus because all day I've been close to tears as others write from their hearts. I'm singing in order not to cry. This is my time to hide, to give myself some breathing room, to think of everything but a bomb and all their grief and helplessness. I can't sing and clap at the same time, but that won't mat-ter. I won't sing with them on Sunday, when we demonstrate what we've been doing. I'll introduce the writers who will read from the work they've shaped in my workshop over the past few days.

Sarah asks me, "Are you going to sing with us on Sunday?" Sarah is the youngest person in my group. She's sixteen; the oldest is seventy-nine. We make quite a crew, sitting in a circle in our trailer, crying and laughing as though it's normal for a seventy-nine-year-old man to write about staying overnight in a convent, as though we can bear Don's tribute to a family whose twenty-year-old son—a bugler in the 19th Kansas Cavalry—was killed in a hunting accident while his regiment was in bivouac in Oklahoma in 1869, testimony to the grief he knows all too well they will never resolve.

"Oh no," I answer. "I can't sing. I'm only having fun."

"Don't you think it's time you did what you're asking all of us to do?" she asks.

What can I do? On Sunday, looking out over scrub oak forests where there is evidence of human habitation for the past 11,000 years, standing beside Lula with my hands held trembling behind my back, I sing.

RED

THREAD. IF YOU TURN YOUR CLOSED EYELIDS TOWARD THE sun, you see blood spin in veins so tiny they color only the dream. Skein of oxygen. It pumps itself up. Heartbeat. Heart beat. Heart break. The valentine cuts itself in two, and your old life folds outward. After. Before. Before you saw red.

Before you were heartsore, red was a wedding, a wine. It sprouted each April, kissing the ground. There, by the fence, an army of red, speaking its mind. Before you were heartsore, you burned at the core all day. You said it oh so carefully in the subjunctive: if red were my color, I'd dance

until dawn. but dancing only happens between griefs, brief as redbud spilling itself on the lawn. I miss the way that dress tied itself around my waist. The day was warm. We walked for miles before the train. At the long-wave end of the spectrum, I twirled on a stick, spun light as cotton candy.

There's an eye watching as I watch. I'm up all night, crossing the continent to meet the rising sun. And when the Chinese fused sunset with flamingo, they let the sky wheel upward in a rush of wings. Transitory. Transitional. A faint implication of color as the redwing settles on the reed.

NOTES

The epigraph is from Dermot Healy's *The Bend for Home,* Harcourt
Brace, 1996. Most of the sources, especially for quotes that func-
tion partially as epigraphs, are indicated in the body of the text.

In "Fred Astaire's Hands," the quoted material from Sylvia Plath is
taken from "Poppies in July" and "Poppies in October," *The Collected
Poems of Sylvia Plath* by Sylvia Plath, © 1981 by the Estate of Sylvia Plath.
Used by permission of HarperCollins.

In "Still Life with Flowers," some of the facts and the anony-
mous Indian quotation come from *Lewis & Clark,* directed by Ken
Burns for the Public Broadcasting System.

The first section of "Out of Place" was dedicated to Stanley W.
Lindberg and the second to my brother George. The essay origi-
nally appeared in *The Georgia Review* with the following Author's
Note:

> Two books: each with a red cover, each with the
> name O'Brien on the spine, so that when I
> reach for one I often find myself holding the
> other. And thus it occurs to me that Edna
> O'Brien's *House of Splendid Isolation* and Tim
> O'Brien's *In the Lake of the Woods,* despite their
> differences in setting and style, have much in

common. They share a peculiar passion: a kind of patriotism that even as it questions itself recognizes that it is capable of a distorting intensity bordering on alienation. They also share the aesthetic need to find a distance that allows for self-exploration. The result is not the kind of imagination we find in Shakespeare's poet, who "gives to airy nothing / a local habitation and a name," but rather one that must balance its "shaping fantasies" with "cool reason." For each, it's a form of imagination built on the tragedy of history as well as the endurance of place. Its roots are in nonfiction as much as they are in narrative fiction.

Some events change a place so utterly that no place is home. In October 1995, by invitation of the Oklahoma Arts Institute, I had the privilege of conducting a writing workshop for survivors of the April 19 bombing of the Alfred P. Murrah Federal Building in Oklahoma City. The program, called "A Celebration of the Spirit," was held at Quartz Mountain. Five of the participants are quoted in the essay that follows.

Biography of a Poetry by Lorrie Goldensohn, © 1991 by Columbia University Press. Reprinted by permission. Other material is found in Elizabeth Bishop's *Brazil*, Time/Life, 1963, and P.K. Page's *Brazilian Journal*, Lester & Orpen Dennys, Ltd., 1987.

The epigraph for "Distance and Direction" is from "The Dead Never Fight Against Anything" by Pattiann Rogers in *Firekeeper: New and Selected Poems*, Milkweed Editions, 1994, © 1994 by Pattiann Rogers. Reprinted with permission of Milkweed Editions.

Quoted material in "Mix and Match" comes from *The Collected Poems of Sylvia Plath*, © 1981 by the Estate of Sylvia Plath, used by permission of HarperCollins; *The Bend for Home* by Dermot Healy, Harcourt Brace, and *The Poems of Gerard Manley Hopkins*, 4th edn., rev. and enlarged (edited by W.H. Gardner and N.H. MacKenzie), Oxford University Press, 1970.

Some of the information in "Alert Bay" can be found in *The American Cetacean Society Field Guide to the Orca* by David G. Gordon and Chuck Flaherty, Sasquatch Books, 1990.

THE COFFEE HOUSE OF SEVENTEENTH-century England was a place of fellowship where ideas could be freely exchanged. The coffee house of 1950s America was a place of refuge and of tremendous literary energy. At the turn of our latest century, coffee house culture abounds at corner shops and on-line. We hope this spirit welcomes our readers into the pages of Coffee House Press books.

OTHER TITLES OF INTEREST
FROM COFFEE HOUSE PRESS

4   3/09

COLOPHON

Distance and Direction was designed at Coffee House Press
in the Warehouse District of downtown Minneapolis.
The text is set in Spectrum with Castellar titles.